ERIC TAYLOR

Progressive Weight Training for Women

A complete guide for fitness and strength

Springfield Books Limited

First published 1992 by Springfield Books Limited,
Norman Road, Denby Dale, Huddersfield HD8 8TH,
West Yorkshire, England

British Library Cataloguing in Publication Data

Taylor, Eric
Progressive Weight Training for Women
I Title
613.7 .

ISBN 1 85688 021 4

Jacket design: Douglas Martin
Inset design: Chris Hand
Illustrations: Barry Davies
Typesetting: Jamesway Graphics, Middleton, Manchester
Printed and bound in Great Britain by Butler and Tanner Ltd,
Frome, Somerset

Acknowledgements

This book is based upon my interest in and research into fitness training and figure development over nearly twenty years, and during that time I have been fortunate enough to receive generous help, advice and encouragement from many like-minded enthusiasts. I should like them all to know how much I have appreciated their help.

My thanks go in particular to Michael Kanyon and Becky Hale of Nautilus Sports/Medical Industries, Independence, Virginia, USA, for allowing me to draw upon their specialist knowledge and for supplying the photographs for the cover and for Chapter 6.

I am most grateful for the use of the studio facilities provided by Mr and Mrs Kay of KL Photographers, York, who provided all other photography. The equipment was provided by Mitchells and Newitts, York, and The York Viking Leisure Centre.

I should also like to thank the following: Marilyn Luscombe, specialist coach at the YMCA, London; Teresa Brookes, Lecturer at Huddersfield Technical College; Chris Haw, Senior Supervisor, and Mrs Christie of The York Viking Leisure Centre; Lisa Barton, member of the British Amateur Gymnastic Team; Frau Marlies Scholtz, Principal of the Model Schools of Cologne, Düsseldorf and Wuppertal.

My special thanks go to Anne Milner, who never fails to produce an immaculate typescript at short notice. And to my wife Sheila who monitored my work so meticulously.

CONTENTS

Introduction

The most surprising thing about weight training in a leisure centre is how enjoyable it is. Whether you are interested in figure development, losing weight, or improving your sport performance – it is not long before you find a completely new reason for regular attendance.

When you step into the cheerful atmosphere of a weight training gym something special happens. There's no competition and no pressure, everyone works at her own pace, there's only enjoyable and steady activity geared to individual ability. Trained supervisors guide you gently through safe exercise routines which progress steadily and measurably as muscular tone and strength improve. Women weight trainers have found that this is a way they can get into shape safely, relatively painlessly and without unduly disrupting their daily lives. Their enthusiasm is infectious and stems from that overall sense of well-being, that good-to-be-alive feeling which comes with the exhilaration of regular exercise – well within your capability. If you are fortunate enough to join such a group you will be made to feel comfortable in what at first sight might seem a strange environment with curious equipment. So if you are harbouring painful memories of being humiliated in the school gymnasium you will find there is nothing at all daunting in the modern leisure centre.

Getting back into shape can of course be done at home, using free weights, as we shall see, but there is much to be said for joining a club and enjoying the support of staff and social contact with other weight trainers.

The benefits of using weight training machines are twofold. Some feel safer using a machine – you can't drop a weight on your foot! But the main benefit is the way the muscles are worked. Nautilus machines were developed as a result of studying the effects of training with barbells. Researchers found that the barbell was not capable of giving direct, balanced and full range resistance. When you lift a barbell you might wobble or cheat by not using both limbs equally or you might shift position slightly each time you lift thus weakening the training effect. Scientists call this 'random torque'. A machine can control the exercise by using direct resistance and eliminating random torque, and it will do this through the full range of possible movement. So a Nautilus machine is a barbell from which the limitations have been removed; an improved barbell capable of providing harder more intense work. When you consider that using machines allows you to systematically train all the major muscle groups safely and completely, it is worth finding a club with such facilities.

The women who do attend weight training clubs speak convincingly of the benefits. Whilst researching this book I spoke to some of them. A 35-year-old mother who goes out to work said: 'It's done a tremendous amount of good to my self-image, as well as making me more efficient in every aspect of my life. I seem able to deal with daily problems more easily so that I'm coping better than before with less effort.' And a single parent in her late twenties said: 'Regular exercise in the weight training club has altered my whole attitude to everything – food, play, work, sex and even my tolerance of others. I have a general feeling of improved physical and mental confidence which has done much to help me through a traumatic period of my life'.

It's easy to understand why women are so enthusiastic about weight training once you listen to what they have to say about the way it has improved the quality of their lives. Many of them talk about the feeling of euphoria they experience immediately after a session and a shower. And they testify to a wide range of other benefits and a genuine sense of achievement. A married teacher who, twice a week, goes straight to the leisure centre immediately school ends, says, 'I feel much younger now, more self-confident, happier with my figure and more alert. I've stopped smoking, no longer take problems to heart, I walk to places instead of taking the car, and I no longer give a damn about the Headmaster! The spin-off benefits are marvellous – incredible. Another thing about weight training is that you don't want to undermine the effort you've put into exercise by being stupid about diet, alcohol and smoking'.

So, it's safe to say that a fitter, healthier and happier future is yours for the taking. Your health and happiness are literally in your own hands. But now is the time for making decisions. Not tomorrow.

We all know the risks we are taking, of sitting at an office desk or behind the wheel of a car all day and then spending the evening slumped in a chair watching television. If we take no regular exercise to offset the effects of this familiar modern routine, our bodies soon reflect the inactivity. Sedentary living leads to ill health. We begin to look jaded and unfit. We age prematurely.

Weight training provides a simple and enjoyable way of avoiding the serious consequences of a sedentary life. Research carried out in medical schools and universities all over the world points to this infallible and safe way of getting into shape and enjoying that real zest for life of our younger days. It does not take long for the convert to weight training to discover too that you wake up in the morning refreshed and full of vitality – feeling good and looking good. Weight training is indeed a rewarding way to fitness.

CHAPTER ONE

What weight training can do for you

At one time or another most women try various forms of exercise programmes, and most would readily admit to giving up after the first rush of enthusiasm has waned. If it is any consolation, men fare no better: in fact the percentage of men who give up is even higher. Consequently a good deal of effort is wasted; the gains made one week can easily be lost in the weeks of inactivity that follow.

All this is understandable. Pressures of various kinds inevitably cause changes in your priorities and taking exercise won't always be number one. Your good intentions may founder on the rocks of family, social and professional commitments.

So what do you need? A way of exercising that does not get pushed to one side; a way that can be easily maintained by busy working wives and mothers alike. Impossible? No! The good news is that research carried out in medical schools, hospitals and university physical education departments throughout the world points to one simple, safe and effective way to get fit and stay fit – weight training.

First of all we must clear our minds of all the myths and misconceptions about the term 'weight training'. It has nothing to do with the competitive sport of weight-lifting nor the activity of body-building. Weight-lifters use heavy weights to develop great strength and muscular bulk which require highly skilled techniques. They are usually competitive; indeed weight-lifting is an Olympic event.

Women body-builders also use heavy weights and follow a strict diet with the aim of improving their aesthetic appearance and developing lean, hard, well-defined muscles. Their harmoniously shaped bodies are presented before a panel of judges in regional and national competitions, presided over by the International Federation of Body Builders. Women's body-building competitions have become increasingly popular in the United States and Europe in recent years and opportunities to win attractive cash prizes in professional contests has contributed to the rapid growth of the sport.

Weight training is quite a different matter. It consists of exercises with weights, such as dumb-bells, barbells and those provided by specialised machines such as Nautilus, offering resistance to muscles used in exercise routines. The weight can be applied to provide both aerobic exercise, demanding a constant supply of oxygen for its maintenance, or anaerobic exercise, which is so strenuous that muscles run short of oxygen and the exercise has to stop. In short, the term weight training generally covers those exercise programmes designed to improve performance in sport and athletics, to develop the basic components of fitness or simply to provide pleasurable physical exercise.

The beneficial effects of this form of training on physical and mental well-being have long been understood: twenty-five centuries ago, Hippocrates, often called the father of modern medicine, extolled the virtues of exercises done with stones held in each hand. And it was he who coined the oft-quoted axiom: 'That which is used develops, and that which is not wastes away'.

Muscles are designed to be exercised. The most effective form of exercise is described by the magic letters PRE – progressive resistance exercise (*see* Chapters 2 and 4). It is a clumsy phrase meaning that exercise must cause muscles to overcome a progressively greater resistance. This can take the form of using weights or machines.

Facts and fallacies

Female and male muscles respond differently to weight training. When men train with heavy weights they develop muscle mass and definition, but such development cannot occur when women exercise with weights. Women's bodies react differently to exercise, it is one of the female characteristics like a smooth complexion, broader child-bearing hips and other distinctive anatomical features. A woman's hormones and shape are just not conducive to building a massive 'muscle-bound' body. However, you can make gains in muscular tone, strength and flexibility by training with weights.

Another fallacy you may have heard about weight training is the old tale that muscles turn to fat when you stop exercising. Rubbish! It is a physiological and biochemical impossibility. If women athletes get fatter as they get older the reason is not that muscles are turning to fat but simply that they are wasting away with inactivity, and the calories they used to burn up are stored as fat in layers over the muscles. Waist, hips and thighs thicken, and the classic pear-shaped form develops. The appetite for food you acquired in more active days has been retained but calories are no longer expended in physical activity. Weight training, combined with a calorie-controlled diet, can soon alter that by accelerating the calorie-burning process. So forget the fallacy of muscles turning to fat and remember instead the benefits derived from a carefully planned weight training programme – a trim, lithesome, fit body.

The benefits

After only a few short weeks women weight trainers find they are enjoying all the bonuses that come from regular exercise. As the United States Surgeon-General reported[†]:

> People who who exercise regularly say they feel better, have more energy, often require less sleep. Regular exercisers often lose excess weight as well as improving muscular strength and flexibility. Many also experience psychological benefits including enhanced self-esteem, greater self-reliance, decreased anxiety and relief from mild depression.
>
> Sustained exercise improves the efficiency of the heart and increases the amount of oxygen the body can process in a given period of time. Compared to non-exercisers, people who engage in regular physical activity have been observed to have a one and a half to two times lower risk of developing cardiovascular disease, and an even lower risk of sudden death.[†]

Obviously everybody's lifestyles are different and will require different levels of fitness, but whatever the specific need for physical development may be, there are weight training exercises which will provide just the right amount of muscular activity required, safely and within your capability. You can tailor your own programme to fit you.

In other words, by selecting the appropriate weight training exercises you can:

- trim off excess fat
- strengthen muscles
- improve the efficiency of your heart
- increase vital capacity of the lungs
- improve your circulatory system
- develop greater reserves of stamina
- improve your skill and performance at work and play
- regain your figure after childbirth

Within the first few sessions you will be surprised by your remarkable progress. Not all of this is the result of increased stamina and strength – some of it is due to the beginner mastering the techniques of lifting weights on machines or barbells; but nevertheless progress will be made quickly at first. It is encouraging. And as time goes by you will see for yourself how well your body responds to training. This gives a great psychological boost and make you more determined to stick with it!

[†]US President's Council on *Physical Fitness and Health*, 1986

A successful conditioning programme

There are seven functions of a comprehensive conditioning programme.

Your programme should:
- be safe
- meet the needs of the individual – young, old, fit or unfit
- be graded to ensure steady progress
- provide exercise which improves cardio-vascular respiratory efficiency
- burn calories as energy fuel
- provide an easy means of monitoring progress
- foster motivation for further effort from the improvements seen

Weight training meets them all!

Enjoying your exercise

You need an enjoyable session of effective exercise about twice a week. But if it is not enjoyable you are not likely to persevere with it, and the more enjoyable it is the more benefit you will derive from it. This is where weight training has the advantage. Some years ago, aerobics and jogging took the world by storm but many people pushed themselves too far and there were some much-publicised horror stories. Seeking a safe alternative to these activities, women turned to weight training. It is essential to have an exercise programme incorporating a regime which progressively and safely overloads all the body systems, and there is no better way of applying such an overload than through weight training. Chapter 3 deals with planning your own programme.

In the years ahead, whether you stay young and fit will depend on how you decide to live. It will mean balancing work with play, activity with relaxation, exercise with rest, and stress with serenity. This is your life. One day, when you reach a great age, the oft-repeated question might be put to you: 'what would you do if you had to do it all again?' What will you say then? Will you perhaps ruefully echo the ironic wit of Eubie Blake, the ragtime pianist who, on his one hundredth birthday, said: 'If I'd known I was going to live so long I'd have taken better care of myself!'

CHAPTER TWO

How weight training works

Few people will have heard of Milo the Greek, but in his day he was a celebrated wrestler, much admired for his physique. His story still serves well to illustrate how progressive weight training works.

When he was a boy, Milo lived on his father's farm and was fond of animals. One day a new calf was born and when the cow had licked it clean the excited young lad was allowed into the cow-shed. Immediately he picked up the warm furry calf and cuddled it to his chest. He loved the doleful-looking, gentle creature and every day after that first morning, he would run to the field, pick up the calf and carry it around the farm. As the calf grew, so did Milo – and so did his muscles, for each day they had to carry a progressively heavier load which taxed them to the limit. Eventually, Milo's name became synonymous with perfect physical development.

Now, the name of Milo is buried in the dust of history, but the principle behind his physical development lives on in its simple clarity. It is called 'the principle of overload' or 'progressive resistance'. Milo lifted a weight which increased gradually, progressively raising the resistance against which his muscle fibres had to work.

As you pick up this book, only a few of the fibres in your hand and arm muscle need to contract, for the effort required is small. Take up a bag full of books, however, and a far greater proportion of your muscle fibres are required to work. The brain sends impulses to the muscles to activate the right number of fibres for the work involved. If you live a fairly sedentary life, you are unlikely to be called upon to lift any really heavy objects and consequently the brain rarely activates more than the few fibres that are needed. Those muscles never fully stimulated remain small and weak, simply through lack of use.

Training with weights makes you use more of your physical potential, a greater proportion of muscle fibres being brought into action. When heavier weights are lifted repeatedly the work is shunted from one set of fibres to another, so that those fatigued have time to recover. Obviously, the heavier the weight, the greater the proportion of muscle fibres involved and therefore fewer are left to relieve those which are fatigued.

After a few repetitions with a heavy weight, the working muscles become so fatigued that they can do no more until they are rested. In the process of recovering they develop in strength and shape to cope with the new work-load. This development against a gradually increased resistance embodies 'the principle of overload' or 'progressive resistance'. Weight training, whether with free weights or machines, is now considered the most efficient way of increasing progressive resistance and improving muscular development.

Changing your shape

The human body is built from different types of tissue; muscle, fat and bone. The shape of your body changes when you alter the proportions of these constituents. Some fat is essential. Though part of it is just 'storage fat', it also has some beneficial functions – protecting organs, insulating the body, storing vitamins and energy. But we all know that when the proportions of fat to bone and muscle go drastically awry, through over-eating and lack of exercise, the body changes shape in a way not altogether pleasing.

Weight training can reverse the process by: using muscles to burn off unsightly storage of fat around hips and thighs, developing more muscles which make for pleasing curves, poise and vitality. Exercises can be done with free weights, machines or both.

Free weights

The term free weights applies to dumb-bells and barbells. Dumb-bells, short bars with a weight attached to each end, are designed to be held in one hand and are generally used in pairs. Barbells are longer metal bars with space for both hands to grip and they have heavier weights attached by screws and collars.

For many of the weight training exercises, dumb-bells and barbells are interchangeable, though each type has its own special advantages. Dumb-bells provide greater flexibility in the range and angle of movement, whilst barbells give you more control when you use them with heavier weights. You will soon discover which feels best for you in a particular range of movements.

A point worth considering about the use of free weights is that they force you to balance your body and the weights for different ranges of movement. This involves a much greater utilisation of your total muscular system – those muscles involved in making the movement, those used in stabilising the joint and also those used for keeping the body balanced (prime movers, stabilisers and synergists). Consequently, improved muscular coordination, developed through the use of free weights, transfers to movements in everyday life, whether for recreation, sport or work activities.

Free weights also allow you to bring into your training programme a greater variety of exercises than the few each machine can provide. Many weight trainers appreciate this as a means of introducing diversity into training schedules over the months and years of exercise.

Free weights can be used at home as well as in leisure centres and gyms. Some women prefer to have their own home gym and train there because they can exercise whenever and for as long as they wish. This does have its advantages, but if you are a beginner seek independent and specialist advice before buying expensive equipment. It is not all made to the same standard. Some barbells, for example, bend when more than two hundred pounds are attached.

Many weights now come in metric calibrations. A simple way of working out the approximate poundage is to multiply by two and add 10 per cent: thus 20kg equals $20 \times 2 = 40 + 10\% = 44$ pounds approximately.

A basic set of free weights for a woman's training schedule could begin with the following:

- two dumb-bell rods and locking collars
- one barbell with locking collars
- disc weights totalling 60kg, say four discs at $2\frac{1}{2}$kg, four discs at 5kg, four discs at $7\frac{1}{2}$kg
- padded bench adjustable for inclined positions.

All this can be expensive. You may find it cheaper – and more enjoyable – to become a long-term member of a gym or leisure centre where you can use machines as well as free weights.

Exercise machines

Exercises on machines, as with those done with free weights, depend for their effects upon the quality of overload or resistance which can be applied to specific muscle groups. Where machines score heavily in this respect, particularly the Nautilus range, is that they can direct the resistance of gravity. Put it this way: when a barbell is used, gravity acts in one direction – downwards – whereas most of the body's movements are in curves of a rotary nature. Consequently, the resistance provided solely by gravity varies as limb joints are flexed. For example, with the simple arm curl exercise, in raising a barbell to the finishing position at the shoulder, gravity imposes a maximum resistance only in the approach to the mid-point of exercise, and for the last third of the movement the arm flexor muscles contract against much less resistance.

Machines used for the same movement can provide a constant pressure throughout the whole range of movement. Alternatively, machines can increase resistance in the range of movement where the muscles are strongest and decrease it where they are weaker.

Coaches and sports scientists who have watched the progress of women weight trainers now seem to favour greater use of exercise machines, for two main reasons. Firstly, they provide a more efficient training effect over a wider range of movement. The notion of efficiency is used here in its precise meaning of producing greater returns for less effort in less time. You can get through a complete work-out in a relatively short session. The second reason is that apart from physiological advantages, Nautilus-type exercise machines are safer to use. You can lose your balance, drop a barbell or dumb-bell on your feet or even get stuck awkwardly and dangerously beneath a barbell when performing a bench press, though such accidents should never happen if you are using proper weight training techniques. Exercise machines, however, make such accidents impossible.

What to wear when training

During the last decade, sportswear seems to have dominated fashion, with a wide variety of bright designer tracksuits and brand-name training shoes. But usually you need not expect to be in competition with trendy fitness enthusiasts in weight training gyms. Wear whatever you feel most comfortable in when you are working hard. Leotards and tights, and clothing with lycra as worn by track athletes and cyclists, have found favour because they allow for freedom of movement, but if you are not comfortable dressed like that then a T-shirt and shorts are acceptable.

Take care to have something warm to wear between exercises. The shell suit was designed specifically for this purpose before it became a major fashion item, and is ideal for stopping you from chilling off.

Shoes are very important. Choose shoes that give support, both in the arch and around the ankle. Do not be tempted to buy expensive shoes simply because they have a well-known name. According to a recent report of the Consumers' Association which investigated some leading brands, most expensive does not necessarily mean best. (*Daily Telegraph*, August 6, 1991)

The advice is to be sceptical of claims about miracle technology or of achieving improvements in sporting performance. There are several brands of shoes, called cross-trainers, designed to suit more than one sport. So if you enjoy running or court activities, as well as weight training, you don't need three or four different types of shoe.

> Here's some advice for choosing your shoes for weight training:
>
> - Wear the same socks as you would when training.
> - Make sure the shoe cups the heel firmly and feels comfortable.
> - Check that it grips the floor and does not slip.
> - Feel for seams inside the shoe which might rub and cause blisters.
> - Look for strong upper and side support: extra stable shoes are desirable for weight training to prevent loss of balance when extra pressure is put on legs and feet.
> - Stand on one foot and then the other when trying on shoes to make sure your foot can spread.

Safety measures

Weight training is one of the safest of all fitness activities, but if you are in any doubt about its suitability for you, seek medical advice. You should consult your doctor before starting any exercise programme if you have ever had high blood pressure or heart disease, severe chest trouble such as bronchitis, severe arthritic pains in joints or back or if you are just recovering from an operation.

It cannot be over emphasized to all weight trainers – men and women – that progression should be gradual and the severity of demands made by the exercise upon your heart and lungs should be carefully regulated.

Women often worry about such hazards as hernia, slipped discs and heart strain, so we will look at these in turn. Hernia, or rupture, occurs when intra-abdominal pressure is raised during lifting. Weakness in the abdominal wall is not necessarily caused by weight training and if any weakness is there, then sooner or later herniation could occur anyway, whether it be in the gym or moving furniture at home.

Another common concern is the risk of a slipped disc or other back trouble. Back pain affects young and old alike. It is a universal woe and it is no consolation to know that four out of five people suffer from it at some time in their lives. In a variety of ways it can begin without warning, it is really brought about by adopting a faulty position when lifting. The maxim for lifting anything heavy, whether a bucket of water or weighted barbell, is 'a firm base and straight back'. Never reach forward with a round back and jerk upwards on a heavy weight, otherwise something will give – usually those small muscles linking the separate segments of the spine. Consequently the soft cartilaginous disc, which acts as a cushion between the bones, may bulge forward, causing painful pressure on the sciatic nerve serving the lumbar region, buttocks and back of the leg.

Prevention is always better than cure. Avoid the causes of back pain. Keep your back and abdominal muscles strong through regular exercise. When lifting weights adopt a position with your feet just underneath the bar. Lower your hips, bend your knees and keep your head up with your back straight. Remember too, lift the weight with your leg muscles and not those of your back.

Finally there is the fear of heart strain. Can weight training cause heart problems? It can, but only in exactly the same way as it would if you had the misfortune to have a puncture and had to struggle with a wheel-brace to loosen nuts that were overtightened by the garage drill. Maximum exertion the pressure inside the chest cavity increases tremaximum exertion the pressure inside the chest cavity increases tremendously. Blood is forced out of the pulmonary vascular system into the arteries, where it joins blood pumped from the heart and the blood pressure in the arteries rises. At the same time, owing to the abnormally high compression within the chest cavity caused by holding the breath during maximum exertion, the blood from the veins is unable to force its way back to the heart. Then the heart is unable to maintain a steady supply to the arteries and blood pressure drops alarmingly – so much so that the pulse beat may disappear altogether. If, when the lift is completed, the breath is released explosively, the heart immediately dilates and there is an enormous rush of blood into its chambers. These sudden changes are dangerous. They can, however, be easily avoided.

Breathe in before you start and breathe out as you make the effort. **Never hold your breath.**

Safety code

There are some risks with every sport. Those for women weight trainers are minimal if this safety code is followed:

- always warm and stretch muscles and joints first
- use the correct technique in all exercises; always remember this maxim – firm base, straight back
- do not train if you feel unwell, or have a cold or viral infection
- progress gradually in poundage and repetitions
- ensure all equipment is properly secure and adjusted
- breathe evenly
- keep to a steady rhythm, never strain or labour jerkily
- stop immediately if training causes nausea or excessive breathlessness

CHAPTER THREE   # Getting started

'A journey of a thousand miles begins with a single step' is a saying we've all heard. And that first step is to make purposeful exercise part of your life. It's going to be something you do regularly, not just now and again, so that it is integrated pleasurably with your work, leisure and social activities. For one of the great benefits of weight training is that because you are feeling fitter you naturally take more exercise. You walk where once you drove, you climb stairs where once you stood in a crowded lift.

We all know, basically, what we want to achieve: a highly efficient, great looking, active body and an alert mind. We know also how easy it is to start a new activity and how difficult it can be to keep it going! But with weight training there are so many added incentives; not only do you quickly feel the benefits but you can see them in the mirror and in your rapid progress through the weights and repetitions.

But a word of warning: do not start too ambitiously, and never push yourself to excess so that you find yourself too tired and stiff to exercise for a day or two. Give yourself time to make progress.

Too old for weight training?

Doctors and physiotherapists who favour weight training as a means of physical rehabilitation all have stories to tell of their successes. Vivian Grisogono,[†] a former Olympic physiotherapist, spoke of one eighty-year-old lady she sees regularly who does stretching exercises and weight training to keep her muscles and joints in good shape for ice skating!

Age should not be considered a barrier to weight training but the older you are the more careful and less ambitious you must be. Check with your doctor first if you have any sign of impaired coronary circulation, as the extra strain due to increased intra-thoracic pressure in lifting weights, might be a serious risk. Then, for your own safety, an alternative physical routine would be better.

Otherwise, for the fit and elderly, as Delorme and Watkins[‡] write: 'A judicious progressive increase in resistance is the most important element in an exercise regime designed to augment strength'. Take care always to warm up with some stretching and mobilising exercises before you start work with weights.

[†]*Daily Telegraph*, 6 August 1991
[‡] *Progressive Resistance Exercise* Thomas DeLorme and Arthur Watkins, Appleton-Century-Crofts, New York, 1951

Warm-up routines

The body needs stretching exercises as well as strengthening ones, otherwise joints, muscles, tendons and ligaments lose their ability to function throughout their full range. But do it gently. You are not aiming to become a contortionist, ballet dancer or top class gymnast, and people who have been leading a fairly sedentary life should not suddenly start doing those rhythmic, mobilising or bouncing exercises in which the weight of the head or limbs is used to increase the range of movement.

Most athletes prefer to warm up for a few minutes wearing several layers of exercise clothing so that the body warms more quickly. To be safe, remember the older you are the longer you need to spend on this initial warm-up routine. In a cool gym too this is particularly important. You can also use a static bike on a low setting to help with the warm up. A thorough warm-up routine not only increases the temperature of the body but also loosens up the muscles, so that they contract and relax more readily in response to signals sent from the central nervous system.

Mobilising exercises

Trunk and arm circling
Stand astride, extend the arms up, hands loosely linked, drop your body forward. Sweep gently sideways and downwards in a circling motion and up to the other side. Do not try too hard to stretch those tight hamstring muscles at the back of your legs, nor should you swing violently as you bend your back. Gently loosen up.

Half knee bends

With your feet about six inches apart, knees bent, swing your arms loosely and rhythmically backwards then forwards and upwards. At the same time bend knees and hips as you would in skiing, straighten the body up as the arms go up and bend down as you take the arms back.

Single leg swinging

Stand erect, sideways on to a chair or wall, rest the fingers of one hand on the back of the chair or against the wall. Raise your outside leg and keeping it straight as possible swing it loosely backwards and forwards. Repeat with the other leg. This exercise stretches the hamstrings: do not do it too violently.

Knee hugging

Stand comfortably balanced, and raise one knee and hug it to your chest. Lower and repeat with the other leg.

Skipping
You can do this without a rope, on the spot.

Body twists
Stand with your feet apart and your arms forward with fingers lightly clenched, at shoulder height. Keeping the body upright, twist round to the right and then to the left. Allow your arms to swing loosely round with your body and turn the head to look as far back as you can.

Stretching exercises

Remember that this is still the warm-up part of the routine – be gentle! Do not be too eager to progress by forcing joints and muscles beyond a comfortable range of movement. Err on the side of safety. Complete each movement as far as the point of sensing a slight discomfort in the joints or muscles that are being stretched. Be patient and be careful.

Forward lunge
Stand with one foot about a pace in front of the other. Bend the knee of the leading leg keeping the back leg straight. Gently press the heel of the rear leg to the floor. Feel the stretch in the calf muscle, then change legs and repeat.

Shoulder stretch
Arms straight behind your back, hands clasped. Push the arms back as far as you can. Hold, then repeat.

Assisted shoulder stretch
This is a slow steady movement. Left arm behind the neck, fingers reaching towards the right shoulder blade. Raise your right arm and gently press downwards on the top of the left elbow so that your fingers reach further down the shoulder. Change arms and repeat.

Hurdle stretch
Sit on the floor, right leg stretched forward, left leg tucked as far back as you can. Let your body lean slightly backwards, supported by the arms. Change legs and repeat.

Chest stretch
Stand with your feet slightly apart, hands lightly clasped behind the back. Draw your elbows and shoulders back, hold, then repeat.

Thigh muscle stretch
Lie on your right side, right arm extended in line with your body, right leg straight. Reach down with your left hand and gently pull your left leg back, bending the knee to draw your heel up to your seat. Feel the stretch in the quadriceps. Hold this position for a few seconds, return to the start position then repeat.
Change sides and repeat.

These mobilising and stretching exercises will make you feel ready to tackle the weight training routine. Some enthusiastic coaches recommend what is called a specific warm up, which involves practising the exercises with very light weights. Once you are proficient without weights you could try it.

When you've done your warm up, you can start the weight training programme.

Planning your training

When preparing a weight training schedule to suit your individual needs, do not be influenced too much by what you see going on around you in the gym. Women take up weight training with various aims in mind: be clear about your own specific requirements. You are not competing with anybody – not even yourself. Build up the demand on your muscles gradually so that you are doing just a little bit more than last time and no more.

People who work themselves into a frenzy of enthusiasm at the start of a fitness campaign rarely carry it through, for no one can sustain such a pitch of dedication for very long. Settle for steady progress with a basic starting schedule, such as one of those given below, and you can concentrate on specific muscle groups and problem areas later.

Initially your weight training schedule should aim to exercise the muscles of the whole body, to ensure harmonious development. You can achieve that if you plan it properly from the outset. To do that you need to decide about: the selection of exercises, the poundage or resistance for each exercise, the number of repetitions to be attempted for each exercise.

All the exercises in the two beginners' schedules which follow will help to develop the efficiency of your heart, lungs and circulatory system. By comprehensively exercising all the major muscle groups you will bring about an energy deficit so that surplus fat is used as energy fuel, thus steadily eliminating that store of fat – known as a spare tyre. The exercise routine should be followed in the order presented below. In this way the muscle groups are worked in turn they complement and reinforce each other without actually duplicating the effort required from each particular muscle groups.

There are three basic grips:
Overgrasp – when the palms of both hands face towards you and the bar is gripped between the fingers and thumbs.

Undergrasp – the direct opposite of overgrasp. The palms of the hands face away from you and come upwards onto the bar with thumbs uppermost and closing on top of it.

Alternate grasp – for some exercises this grasp might be used to achieve specific effects. Here one hand takes the overgrasp and the other the undergrasp.

In all three lifting grips the hands are usually kept a little wider than shoulder width apart. With this position the arms drop comfortably on either side of the knees when you adopt the crouch position to pick up a barbell from the floor.

Exercise positions

The basic lifting positions are defined here. Please make sure you are familiar with them before you start.

Standing erect

Feet approximately shoulder width apart, toes pointing forwards and only slightly outwards, instep immediately below the barbell, heels flat on the floor.

Crouch position

Start from standing position, with feet well under the bar, bend at the hip, knee and ankle to grasp the bar. Keep the back as straight as possible, arms straight and just outside the knees. Head up.

Barbell on chest

This is the start position for many arm and shoulder exercises. With feet roughly shoulder width apart, pick up the barbell with overgrasp and raise it until it lies across the upper part of the chest, elbows pointing downwards and as close to the side as is comfortable.

Shoulder rest

With feet roughly shoulder width apart, pick up the barbell with overgrasp raise it overhead, then lower it gently behind your head to lie across the back of neck and shoulders: draw the shoulders well back.

Beginners' schedule with free weights

1 *Warm-up and stretching*

2 *Overhead barbell press*

Sometimes called the 'military press', this exercise helps to strengthen the frontal fibres of the deltoid muscles and the shoulder girdle itself.

Adopt an erect standing position, back straight, barbell on chest starting position. Keeping the legs and back straight, press the barbell directly overhead, arms fully extended. Lower slowly to starting position (*See* page 44).

3 *Undergrasp arm curl*

This arm movement (sometimes called the biceps curl) is a simple exercise for developing the arm and shoulder muscles generally and the biceps in particular.

From the standing erect starting position, undergrasp, with the barbell across the front of the thighs, arms straight by the sides. Curl the barbell upwards to the chest, keeping elbows close to the sides and lower slowly to the starting position. By lowering the weight slowly you give more work to the arm flexors thus lengthening the muscles. Avoid leaning backwards and swinging the weighted bar up: this will put a strain on the back.

4 *Half squat*

This exercise is much favoured for strengthening and firming up the quadriceps. It is also a most beneficial exercise in burning off fat as energy fuel, for the leg muscles comprise two-thirds of the body's total muscle mass. You are not only developing tone and strength in thigh and hip muscles but also shedding fat in the process.

Stand with barbell in shoulder rest position, bend your knees until your thighs are approximately parallel to the floor and stretch up into the standing position. Try to avoid dropping into a full knee bend position, which puts extra strain on to the knee joint.

5 *Bent arm raise or fly*

There are several terms used to describe this exercise in which dumbbells are used to develop the pectoral muscles, which lie under the breasts. The exercise improves overall chest expansion and the fibres of the pectoral muscles become broader and new capillaries open up to feed the muscle. The increased blood supply carries vital energy fuel and tissue-building material to the working muscles. Protein from the diet is utilised for new tissue growth and thus the contour of the muscle improves.

Lie on a bench, hold dumb-bells with your arms slightly bent, elbows pointing towards the floor, and palms of the hands uppermost. Raise both arms together until they are above your shoulders and then lower them slowly. Let the arms hang well down below the shoulders before raising them.

A variation to this exercise is to bring the arms upwards and right across the body until the knuckles of each hand approach the opposite shoulder. This crossover action is particularly beneficial for the upper fibres of the pectoral muscles of the chest.

6 *Trunk curl*

The best exercises for rehabilitating weak abdominal muscles and also for strengthening those already in good shape, are those which work the muscles when shortened – usually by curling the body. There are three main muscles: the recti abdominis, the obliques (internal and external) and the transversalis. These are vital muscles that give the multi-way stretch support to your abdomen as well as providing power to turn and twist the trunk.

There is one vital principle to remember – never work abdominal muscles when they are stretched. This means the old-fashioned exercise of lying on your back with both legs straight then raised is taboo.

Lie on your back with knees raised, feet flat on the floor, hands by your sides, head and shoulders raised slightly. Curl forwards and upwards to touch your kneecaps with both hands.

When you are stronger you can try the variation of trunk curl with twist. Clasp the hands behind the head. As you curl up try to touch your right knee with the left elbow, return to lying position, then curl up again to touch the left knee with right elbow. Doing this throws more work upon the internal and external oblique muscles. (*See also* page 46.)

7 *Bent-over rowing*

This is an essential exercise for women who spend much of their time, every day, working at a desk, computer or bent over a table. Consequently in these long periods when the back is slightly bent forwards, the dorsal muscles have to work in a lengthened position to maintain the body's balance and they eventually become both weaker and longer. In extreme cases, with older women, the postural defect of the dowager's hump can develop. If rehabilitation exercise is delayed, bony and ligamentous changes can make the condition chronic and beyond response to exercise. (*See also* Chapter 11.)

Systematic exercise, using light weights at first, can restore muscular balance between opposing muscle groups of the back and shoulder and greatly improve posture. The bent-over rowing exercise is particularly good for muscles of the upper back.

Select a fairly heavy dumb-bell. Lean forward at the waist with o. foot about half a pace in front of the other. Place the free hand on the forward knee. Support the upper body firmly on this non-working arm. Hold the dumb-bell in the other hand, bend and stretch the arm to bring the dumb-bell well back – as far beyond the shoulder as possible. Repeat as many times as is comfortable, then change position and work the other side.

A variation is to rotate the torso slightly when pulling the dumb-bell back to work the oblique abdominal muscles. (*See* page 53.)

8 *Side bending*

This exercise complements the work done by the dorsal and abdominal muscles in the two previous exercises.

Stand with your legs about a pace apart, hold a dumb-bell in each hand, and bend rhythmically at the hips from left to right, keeping your body in the same erect plane. Do not use weights which are so heavy as to affect the smoothness of movement. A violent swinging of the body sideways using heavy weights can do more harm than good. In this exercise it is important that you avoid bending forwards or backwards from the hips. (*See* page 54.)

9 *'Heavy hands' running on the spot*

By the time you reach this exercise, the previous physical activity will already have raised your heart rate and provided a good conditioning routine for the cardio-vascular system. The final exercise in this set of eight will help to promote further a feeling of general warmth and an increase in the rate and depth of respiration.

Hold a light disc weight in each hand, arms hanging loosely. Run gently on the spot, flexing and stretching the ankles for about a minute. Allow the shoulders to shrug freely. Rest for two or three minutes before starting the exercises again.

For guidance on how many sets of exercises and repetitions you should attempt in this free weights routine, see Chapter 4.

Selecting the system

Few women today would argue with a statement made in the recent survey, sponsored by the Sports and Health Education Councils, which said: 'Most people don't want to be super-fit. They want to be able to enjoy life to the maximum with minimum amount of effort.'[†]

But how do we know what the minimum amount of effort is in weight training terms? Quite simply, beginners should follow either of the free weights schedules suggested in chapter 3, or one on machines, or a combination of both, and then you can decide on the best system to use. The intensity of the exercise and its duration are as shown below.

How much should you do?

The intensity of your exercise routine depends upon the poundage that your muscles have to work against and the number of times the exercise is repeated.

Try each exercise first with weights light enough for you to handle easily and correctly. Then, after a short rest, add more weight until you can do no more than ten repetitions (usually called reps). Take care! Avoid the temptation of being too ambitious and adding extra weight before you are ready. You should not be straining to complete the last of the ten repetitions. Keep progress within the range of comfortable minimum effort. Increase your repetitions to at least twelve or thirteen before adding more weight or resistance to the exercise movement. In fact, in the early stages of training, there is much to be said for exercising with light weights and doing a much higher number of repetitions for each exercise in the set. Initially your set could consist of six to eight different exercises to make a routine.

Exercise with lighter weights and a high number of repetitions, say twenty, will develop muscular endurance, whereas heavier weights and few repetitions, say about six, will develop strength and power.

Both heavy and light weight routines can effectively improve cardio-vascular fitness provided the exercise does raise the heart rate to a high level and sustain it for between fifteen and thirty minutes.

[†]*Getting Into Shape* by Gay Search and David Denison, New English Library, 1988

Which system should you choose?

Different coaches have their own variations on the basic methods or systems of training and are likely to argue their merits in highly technical terms. So some physiological explanations have been included with the description of the basic systems given below.

It must be said that despite all the scientific research which has taken place in the field of exercise physiology during the last twenty years, there is still a divergence of opinion on these basic systems of training. The reason for this is that although training records show clearly the time spent, the severity and duration of the exercise, the poundage, repetitions and sets used, they do not show one vitally important factor – motivation. As you would expect, the determination and enthusiasm of the individual concerned has a marked effect upon progress. So my advice is simple: select the system that suits you best. Tackle it with enthusiasm and it will repay your efforts.

The circuit system

The circuit or sequence system is enjoying new-found favour in gyms and leisure centres, because it can be easily designed to suit each individual. It could, for example, be biased mainly towards cardio-vascular fitness and endurance – using high repetitions, light weights and shorter rest breaks between sets – or it could be aimed at developing muscular size and shape. (*See also* Chapter 7.)

As the name implies, circuit training involves going round a circuit or sequence of exercise stations one after another, with hardly a pause in between. You do a set number of repetitions of each one until you come to the first exercise again, and then, if you are feeling fit enough, you do a second lap.

The task or set number of repetitions to be done at each exercise station is decided by a simple test before you start your training session. Do try out the exercises first, so that you get the feel of them, before you begin to test yourself on each exercise. At first you might find the movements a little awkward, but with practice the technique will come, so that when you do actually test yourself you will get an accurate picture of your state of fitness.

Take each exercise in turn and see how many repetitions of each one you can do before fatigue makes you falter. This is the time to stop and record your score. Do not strain for one more repetition merely to make up a 'round number'.

The task for each training session should then be set at half the maximum number of repetitions achieved, and ideally two laps of the circuit should be done at this rate. For those who are already fairly fit, the task should be set at two-thirds of the maximum number of repetitions achieved at each exercise and three laps completed.

The order of exercises should always be arranged so that different parts of the body are exercised in rotation, so that the major muscle groups have time to recover before they are worked again. Remember that no matter how fit you might once have been, you should not push yourself too hard at first. If you begin training at a comfortable rate then you are more likely to keep up the training sessions. Circuit training can be very strenuous, so take it easy at first and warm-up well before each session.

The triple set system

When equipment is limited or restricted to free weights only, then the triple set system can be useful, both for beginners and those in more advanced stages of training. Its merit lies in the fact that by doing three sets of repetitions for the exercise, one after the other with a recuperative pause in between each set, there is no need to move frequently from one piece of apparatus to another. Furthermore, there is no need to adjust the weight of resistance until you start the next exercise. The number of repetitions for each exercise depends on whether you are aiming for strength or stamina. A poundage heavy enough to keep the repetition below ten is used for strength development, and a lighter poundage, allowing twenty or more rapid repetitions, for stamina.

Making progress

Progress with weight training should be carefully monitored, whether you are using circuit training or the triple set system. Progress with both systems can be achieved by adding more weight (increasing the resistance on machines), or by increasing the number of repetitions, depending upon the aims of your own programme. So if you want to improve the efficiency of your heart, lungs and circulation, then observe the following guidelines:

- take little or no rest between exercise stations
- do many laps of the circuit
- do a high number of reps with light weights at each station

If your aim is mainly for strength and muscle development, then the following is more appropriate:

- use heavier weights with fewer repetitions

- do no more than two laps of the circuit
- rest for 1-2 minutes between stations

When you have only a limited amount of time, then you may have to compromise between different methods of training. But try not to make a habit of it!

For those who wish to improve specific performance in athletics or sport, there are advanced training techniques which can be introduced into the basic schedule. These are explained in Chapters 7, 8 and 9.

Overloading

When you systematically overload a muscle, its individual fibres increase in size and strength. Furthermore, physiologists claim that overloading improves the control of the muscle by the nervous system because motor impulses can be discharged into a trained muscle at a greatly increased frequency and so stimulate a higher proportion of fibres into a stronger contraction. With increased strength and improved nervous control, the trained muscles show a marked improvement in endurance and strength.

Although not many women want great muscular strength, moderate strength can nevertheless be an asset in everyday life. Look at it this way – work which was once arduous can be done more easily and you can finish the day less tired and with energy to spare. There is also a psychological benefit that comes with improvement in strength and stamina. You feel more confident in what your body can do and consequently you are less afraid of making increased demands upon it.

How fit do you want to be?

If you start panting hard before you get to the top of the second flight of stairs, something is wrong. You are drastically out of condition. You know, furthermore, that it is often a self-inflicted condition, caused by a lack of physical activity, perhaps through smoking and probably through overeating. And so you do something about it – you begin a conditioning programme.

When you have reached your goals regarding fitness and figure your next aim is to maintain all that you have achieved so far. But you may wonder how fit you need to be?

Your fitness is relative to the amount of activity you do, and rarely do we know how fit we are – where we rank in the acceptable general level of fitness which doctors describe as the capacity of the heart and muscles to use oxygen efficiently for energy production. To find out how fit you are, relative to other people, try these tests.

Your heart rate

To get a simple guide to your relative cardio-vascular fitness, count your pulse rate before and after taking exercise. Compare your figures with those in the charts below.

Resting heart rate for women

Age	20–25	30–39	40–49	50+
Excellent	71	71	73	75 or less
Good	72-77	72-79	75-79	77-83
Fair	78-95	80-97	80-98	84-102
Poor	96+	98+	99+	103+

If you feel fit enough to test yourself further, then you can try the step test. It is research-proven way of measuring aerobic or cardio-vascular fitness, but it can be very demanding upon your heart, lungs and legs. Do not complete it if you feel it is too much for you. You will need a firm box or stool about 8″ high and a timer with a second hand.

The step test

1 Step onto the box, with alternate feet – left up, right up, left down, right down.
2 Keep to a rhythmic pace of about twenty-four step-ups a minute.
3 Do this for three minutes without stopping.
4 After three minutes of stepping, stop. Sit down. Rest for thirty seconds: take your pulse for the next thirty seconds. Count the number of beats, multiply this figure by two, to get your heart recovery score.
5 Consult the table below to find your fitness grade.

Your fitness guide

Age	20–29	30–39	40–49	50+
Excellent	86	86	88	90
Good	99-110	95-112	96-114	100-116
Fair	99-110	95-112	96-114	100-116
Poor	112+	114+	114+	118+

Another useful tip about your pulse rate is to take it after you have been exercising for ten or fifteen minutes so that you know what your maximum heart rate is after hard work. You should not push yourself so hard that your heart is beating greatly above the optimum rate. You should not exceed this optimum or 'target zone' for your own heart rate. The safe target zone can easily be set by deducting your age from 220. Thus, if we look at the chart we can see that at the age of forty your maximum heart rate would be no more than $220-40=180$ beats per minute, and your target zone rate for exercise would be between 60 per cent and 85 per cent of this figure of 180, giving a target zone of between 108 and 153 beats per minute.

Your exercise heart rate

Age	maximum heart rate (beats per minute) (220 minus your age)	target zone	
		60%	85%
25	195	117	166
30	190	114	162
40	180	108	153
50	170	102	145
60	160	96	136
65+	155	93	132

It's never too late, but ...

Throughout this chapter on training systems and progress, the point has often been made, and it cannot be stressed too much, that you must take care. Start moderately. If you have not taken much exercise over the past few years, then both cardiac and skeletal muscles will have deteriorated. They will have lost strength and bulk. Muscles not used atrophy or shrink.

People lose muscle bulk and tone as they grow older and they accept the condition as a necessary part of ageing. But this is not so. Loss of muscle bulk is the result of under-use and not an automatic consequence of advancing years. Fortunately, both the heart and skeletal muscles respond rapidly to progressive resistance exercises, no matter how weak and atrophied they have become through disuse. Have faith. The loss of muscle strength and bulk is not irreversible. After a few weeks of careful weight training, muscles will be rehabilitated – they will develop in size and power. And remember too that because women have fewer muscle fibres than men, their potential for the development of those bulging muscles seen on men's body-building advertisements is negligible.

Be businesslike. You are managing the most important thing in your life – your health. Keep a weekly record of what you have done. Make time for your training each week so that it becomes a habit. Then you will achieve your aims and objectives – a highly efficient, great-looking active body and alert mind. This quote from a thirty-year-old woman illustrates the point vividly: 'I started weight training in winter and when the summer holidays came round I hit that beach with a shapely silhouette and was absolutely fizzing with energy.'

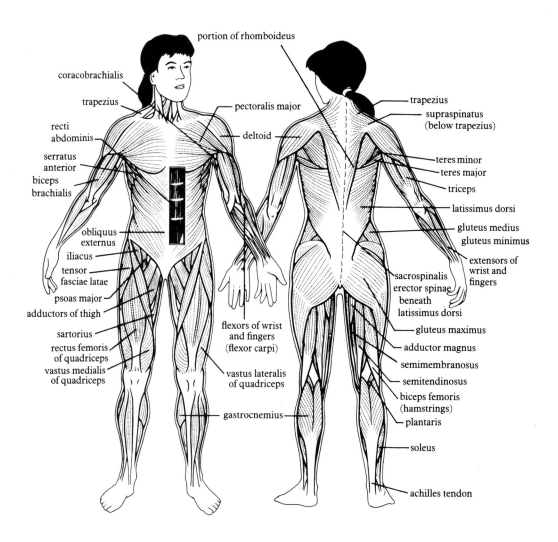

portion of rhomboideus

coracobrachialis

trapezius

recti abdominis

serratus anterior

biceps brachialis

obliquus externus

iliacus

tensor fasciae latae

psoas major

adductors of thigh

sartorius

rectus femoris of quadriceps

vastus medialis of quadriceps

pectoralis major

deltoid

flexors of wrist and fingers (flexor carpi)

vastus lateralis of quadriceps

gastrocnemius

trapezius

supraspinatus (below trapezius)

teres minor

teres major

triceps

latissimus dorsi

gluteus medius

gluteus minimus

extensors of wrist and fingers

sacrospinalis erector spinae beneath latissimus dorsi

gluteus maximus

adductor magnus

semimembranosus

semitendinosus

biceps femoris (hamstrings)

plantaris

soleus

achilles tendon

CHAPTER FIVE

Exercises with free weights for the major muscle groups

The weight training exercises described in this chapter have been specially selected, from the hundreds of variations that exist, as those which are most suitable for women.

Women beginning weight training are sometimes nervous about exercising with free weights. Coordination, balance and correct breathing are important. Handling dumb-bells and barbells is a skill which has to be learnt, and at first you may feel more at ease with the Nautilus machines for women featured in Chapter 6. However, bringing free weights into your weight training programme has definite benefits. At first the beginner might feel wobbly and uncoordinated but after a few sessions you will cope confidently with both dumb-bells and barbells. It is not difficult to design a personal schedule for developing muscle strength, improving tone, shedding weight or improving performance in sport and athletics.

The exercises are classified according to the major muscle groups involved in the movements and arranged in a sequence in which they would usually appear in the schedule. Use your own judgement to choose exercises to suit your own requirements, listening of course to the advice of a qualified supervisor in the gym, if available. The diagram across the page shows you the location of the muscle groups mentioned in each exercise.

Use light weights at first with a low set of repetitions and take care to observe always the safety principles outlined in Chapter 2 and the correct lifting technique.

Lifting technique

Your spine is not designed to carry heavy loads when it is in a horizontal or rounded position. It works most efficiently and with least risk of damage when it is upright, held straight by the postural muscles. The weight of the body and any load carried can then be transmitted directly through the vertebrae and cartilaginous shock-absorbing discs to the supporting pelvis and legs. The technique is the same whether you are lifting a barbell or a heavy box.

When lifting if the back is rounded and the leg muscles are working hard, a greater load is thrown upon the smaller muscles of the spine. Sometimes these muscles, which hold the vertebrae together, are not equal to the task and injury results.

> Specialists who have studied the mechanics of muscle action have recommended the following as the correct technique for lifting:
>
> 1 keep the back as straight as possible
> 2 use the powerful leg extensor muscles
> 3 position your feet under the bar and about 12-18 inches apart
> 4 squat down to take hold of the bar
> 5 keep the combined centre of gravity of your body and the load directly over your feet as you lift
> 6 breathe freely throughout the movement

If you keep your dorsal and abdominal muscles strong through regular exercise you are unlikely to have any problems with your back: prevention is better than cure. So now you have started weight training, remember to correctly lift, then lower the weight to the ground on every occasion, without fail, however light the weight, until the technique becomes automatic.

Now for the exercises themselves. Read the descriptions carefully; do not merely glance at the photographs.

Arm and shoulder exercises

Arm curls *(with barbell)*

Muscle groups: arm flexors
Major muscles: biceps brachialis

Stand with your feet 12-18 inches apart and take up the barbell in the manner described above. Hold it with the palms forward, undergrasp, arms straight down so that the bar lies across the front of your thighs. Keeping your upper arms still and close to your body, slowly bend your elbows to bring the bar up to the shoulder. Return the bar slowly, controlling the pull of gravity, to the starting position. Straighten your arms completely at the end of the movement. Repeat. Try to avoid leaning back at the hips to import leverage and swing to the movement. Keep wrists straight.

Reverse curls

These are performed in exactly the same way as arm curls, but with hands in the overgrasp position.

Single arm curls *(with dumb-bells)*

Muscle groups: arm flexors
Major muscles: biceps brachialis

You can use the dumb-bells either both together or alternately in a continuous motion. If one arm is weaker than the other, arm curls will eventually develop strength equally in both arms.

Stand comfortably astride, holding a dumb-bell in each hand. Alternately bend the right and left arms, bringing the dumb-bell to the shoulder. This causes the postural muscle groups to work more

statically, to support and steady the body during the rhythmical flexing of the arms and is consequently an aid to good carriage and graceful movement of the body, in sport as well as everyday situations.

Wrist curl *(with dumb-bell or barbell)*

Muscle groups: wrist flexors
Major muscles: flexor carpi muscles

This exercise strengthens the wrist flexor muscles; eventually you will improve both your grip and wrist flexion. Sit holding a dumb-bell or barbell, resting your forearms on your knees. Flex the wrists upwards and towards the body. Lower as far as possible with wrist fully extended. Repeat over the full range of movement, keeping the forearms still all the time.

Upright rowing *(with barbell)*

Muscle groups: shoulder abductors
Major muscles: deltoid, biceps brachialis, supraspinatus

This is a good exercise for developing and shaping the muscles of the shoulders and upper back. Some women want to increase shoulder width to balance a wide pelvis; this exercise will give a more pleasing rounded line to angular shoulders.

With feet comfortably apart, take up the bar, overgrasp, hands close together, and lift it until the bar lies across the thighs, arms straight. Pull the bar up to chin height, lower slowly and under control to the starting position. Repeat.

Lateral raise *(with dumb-bells)*

Muscle groups: arm abductors
Major muscle: deltoid

This exercise strengthens and shapes the deltoids, which form a 'cap' to the shoulder, and those of the upper back.

Stand with a dumb-bell held overgrasp in each hand, palms towards the hips. With arms straight, lift the dumb-bells sideways to shoulder height and lower to the sides. Breathe evenly, inhaling on the upward movement and exhaling on the downward. Try to keep your body still throughout the movement.

Triceps extension *(with barbell)*

Muscle groups: arm extensors
Major muscles: triceps

For this exercise it is a good idea to perfect the technique with light weights before trying it with heavy weights. A partner can help by assisting with the lift at the back of the neck, where your leverage is weakest. Some women prefer to do this exercise seated.

Hold the barbell in overgrasp, hands a little less than shoulder width apart, the bar resting behind the neck across the shoulders, elbows pointing upwards. Straighten your arms to press the bar to full extension position overhead, with elbows locked. Press your elbows inwards throughout this movement. Lower to the starting position following the same path of movement.

This exercise can be done with dumb-bells, as shown here, exercising one arm at a time or both together. Try to keep your upper arm close to your ear as you lift the dumb-bell

The triceps exercise is one of many free weight exercises which can also be done in a smoother, more controlled way on the Nautilus machine. (*See* Chapter 6.)

Press behind the neck *(with barbell)*

Muscle groups: arm abductors, arm extensors
Major muscles: deltoid, triceps

Grasp the barbell, hands a little more than shoulder width apart. Lift up the barbell, using correct technique, to a position across your chest, press upwards and lower down to the starting position, with the barbell behind the neck and shoulders. Press upwards to the stretch position and lower slowly behind the neck again. Carefully control the descent of the bar to avoid bruising your spine – a towel slung around your neck can be an effective pad. This exercise is often done sitting on a bench.

Military or overhead press *(with barbell)*

> *Muscle groups: arm extensors, arm abductors*
> *Major muscles: triceps, trapezius, deltoid*

Overgrasp, hands shoulder width apart, hold the barbell across your chest at shoulder height. Push the barbell upwards with some momentum until the elbows lock. Take care to push directly upwards so that the weight does not go forwards, thereby upsetting your balance and bringing other muscle groups into play. Lower the bar back to your chest slowly. Keep your body upright and knees straight throughout the exercise. If you wish to vary the resistance and exercise the triceps, pectorals and deltoids as well, do some repetitions with a wide grasp and some with a narrower one.

Overhead dumb-bell press *(with barbell)*

> *Muscle groups: shoulder abductors, elbow extensors*
> *Major muscles: deltoid, triceps*

You can do this exercise seated or standing. Hold the dumb-bells at shoulder height, one at each side. Firmly press the weights upwards, lifting together until they are overhead. If heavy dumb-bells are used, try to have a partner – a 'spotter' – ready to assist in case of difficulties. You can be at some risk when working with heavy dumb-bells overhead.

If your arm and shoulder muscles are weaker on one side than the other, try using dumb-bells for the overhead press as a means to symmetrical development in strength and shape.

Dumb-bell presses can also be done on an inclined bench to vary the resistance placed on the deltoids in the same way that Nautilus machines so easily do. The muscle action involved in the overhead press exercise is the perfect complement to the lateral raise. Together they provide a very good shoulder muscles work-out.

Abdominal exercises

You must be careful to ensure that the abdominal muscles are given correct and balanced training or you can do more harm than good. Weakened and stretched abdominal muscles have to be restored to their former length before being subjected to strenuous resistance exercises. Even then care should be taken to do only those given specialist approval. Some of the exercises often described as 'tummy trimmers' are either futile or harmful. For example, one of these exercises, frequently used to illustrate a reducing regime, is the one in which both legs are kept straight, then raised and lowered from a lying position. Yet this exercise has been condemned for years by physiotherapists and remedial gymnasts because it works mainly the hip muscles and can harm weakened abdominals working hard to maintain a fixed base from which the hip flexor muscles can work.

The exercises recommended below will help to strengthen and restore muscle tone to weakened abdominals. The exercises within the inner range of movement, such as trunk curls, are the most suitable for the safe development of strong abdominal muscles.

It is worth noting the difference between a trunk curl and a sit-up. In the trunk curl, the body is curled forward and upwards by the abdominals and hip flexors, whereas in the sit-up the back is kept straight and the prime movers in the exercise are the hip flexor muscles, psoas major and iliacus.

Some of the exercises which follow use the weight of the body instead of barbells or dumb-bells. A disc weight can be held to increase the resistance offered to the abdominals and hip flexor muscles.

Trunk curl with bent knee

Muscle groups: hip flexors, trunk flexors
Major muscles: psoas major, rectus abdominis, obliques

Lie flat on the floor, bend your knees. Curl your body forward, reaching forward with your hands to let them slide over the tops of your knees. Repeat.

As a progression, try the exercise with arms bent and fingertips touching the side of your head.

Trunk twisting and lowering backwards

Muscle groups: hip flexors, trunk flexors, trunk rotators
Major muscles: psoas major, rectus abdominis, obliques

Sit on the floor with legs comfortably apart. Twist your body to one side as far as you can without undue strain and lower your body to the ground, chin just touching the floor. Sit up and lower your body to the other side. Repeat until you have completed as many movements as possible. Do not worry if you cannot get far round and do not force your body round more than is comfortable.

Trunk curl with twist, legs raised

This exercise is particularly good for developing the internal and external oblique muscles of the abdomen, thus helping to keep organs in place within the abdominal cavity and flattening the stomach.

Lie with the lower part of your legs resting on a bench or chair and with thighs vertical, fingertips touching the side of your head. Curl forwards and upwards, and at the same time twist your body so that your left elbow approaches your right knee. Then, very slowly, lie back down in an uncurling movement. Repeat, twisting in the opposite direction.

Inclined curl or cruncher

When the curl with legs raised becomes easier, then try it with a twist on an inclined bench, feet fixed under a strap. Eventually you can progress to holding a light disc weight behind your head as you curl forwards and upwards to press your head close to your knees.

Leg exercises

Leg exercises form an important part of all women's weight training programmes, for they bring many muscle groups together in one forceful, highly coordinated action.

A word of reassurance will not come amiss here, for some women fear that when thigh muscles develop in strength they will also greatly increase in size. There is no need for such anxiety. Exercises such as the squat and lunge will burn off thigh fat and replace it with shapely muscle.

Squats are most useful too, as we have already seen, for developing cardio-vascular efficiency, and also as a general conditioning exercise – the movements involve not only the major muscle groups of the legs but also, in a secondary capacity, the major muscle groups of the abdomen and back. Consequently squats are an indispensable part of a weight training schedule.

The squat jump *(with dumb-bells)*

Muscle groups: hip and knee extensors
Major muscles: quadriceps, gluteals, erector spinae

Stand with one foot slightly in front of the other and lower your body into a semi-crouch position, dumb-bells held by your side. Now leap forcefully upwards, extending your legs fully, and in mid-air change over the position of your feet. Try to extend your whole body – back, neck and hips. Repeat as many times as possible, with correct positions of body and legs.

The squat *(with barbell)*

Muscle groups: hip and knee extensors, back extensors
Major muscles: quadriceps, gluteals, erector spinae

There are many variations of this knee-bending exercise – back squat, half or partial squat – but the same safety precautions apply. Note them carefully.

- Brace your back as straight as possible.
- Keep the weight well back and not forward of your ankles.
- Sink slowly into the crouch position and do not bounce.
- Avoid bending the knees fully.

When using a heavy barbell, as you will be doing in the squat, you must take care to avoid putting excessive strain on your back muscles, so keep your back straight and do not lean forward at the waist. The knee joint is particularly susceptible to injury. When a heavy weight is put upon the fully flexed joint, ligaments can get pulled.

Half or partial squat

The partial squat is favoured by many weight trainers. In addition to being a safer exercise, a heavier weight can be handled if the knees are not fully bent on lowering the weight. A bench or chair can be used to indicate the lowest point of the knee bend: stop when you feel your bottom touching it, do not sit down! This also ensures that the weight is lowered for the same distance on each knee flexion.

When rising from the squat, try to keep your body positioned correctly all the time; to avoid leaning forward, think about arching your back and pushing your hips forward.

Back squat

Hold the barbell across the back of the shoulders, forearms vertical above your elbows, hands slightly away from the shoulders. Feet should be comfortably apart. If you find it better to have your heels slightly raised then support them with a disc weight or inch (3cm) thick board. Bend at the hips and knees until the upper leg is approximately parallel to the floor. Thrust powerfully upwards, exhaling forcibly at the same time. Repeat as many times as you can.

This is a very valuable exercise, but you must make sure you do it correctly to avoid the risk of injury. When heavy weights are used you will need a spotter standing ready to assist in controlling the weight in case you lose your balance or find yourself unable to get up from the crouch position.

Front squat

Hold the barbell at shoulder height across your chest. Lower the body slowly into the knee bend position, with the upper leg parallel to the ground. Drive forcibly upwards to the standing position, still holding the bar firmly across your chest.

All three squat exercises develop muscle power in the legs, vital for everyday activities as well as sport. Rarely does anyone have need to spring upwards, in sport, from the full knee bend position.

The lunge *(with dumb-bell)*

Muscle groups: quadriceps
Major muscles: quadriceps, gluteus maximus

Stand, holding dumb-bells in each hand, palms towards the sides, feet slightly apart. Take a pace forward and sink slowly into the knee bend position. Let the leading knee go no further forward than the toes of the leading foot. Return to the erect start position by pushing upwards and backwards with the leading foot and stepping back. You may need to take two smaller backward steps with the leading foot to get you into the starting position again.

The lunge variation

Select a light barbell and hold it across your shoulders, low down at the back of the neck. Feet should be about 12 inches apart, toes pointing forward. Step forward a full pace, bending the leading leg so that the knee is slightly ahead of the foot. Extend the rear leg as straight as possible. Push back to return to the start position.

There are several variations of the lunge exercise. You could step forward instead of back to regain the starting position – some women find this easier. Sometimes the rear leg may be bent and sometimes kept as straight as possible, and you can do the exercise with dumb-bells as shown here.

Step-ups

Muscle groups: extensors of the hips, knees and ankles
Major muscles: gluteus maximus, semitendinosus, semimembranosus, quadriceps, soleus, gastrocnemius

Stand facing a firm bench. Step onto the bench with the left foot leading and then step down again, leading with the left foot. Step up and down as many times as possible within thirty seconds; later on, you can try sixty seconds. Weight may be carried once you are really fit!

Leg extension *(with ankle weights)*

> *Muscle groups: knee extensors*
> *Major muscles: quadriceps*

Sit with body leaning backwards and supported on your elbow. Raise the upper part of the right leg with the lower leg parallel to the floor. Extend the leg upwards. Vary the final angle of the extended leg so that sometimes the heel is closer to the floor than shown in the picture. Change legs and repeat.

An easier variation of the leg extension is to sit on a bench with both legs bent to a position halfway between a right angle and the full extension. From this position straighten the weighted legs until they are completely braced.

Make sure you exercise through the full range of movement, extending the leg completely, locking straight at the top for a pause before allowing your leg or legs to return to the starting position.

Leg curls – standing and lying *(with ankle weights)*

> *Muscle groups: knee flexors*
> *Major muscles: biceps femoris, semimembranosus*

Stand with one hand against a support to maintain balance. Bend the weighted leg backwards, ankle until the heel approaches the back of the thigh. Lower slowly down.

A variation is the lying leg curl. Lie face downwards on a bench, weighted bands around each ankle. Bend the knee backwards, keeping the knee and upper thigh firmly on the bench. Lower slowly to the extended position. In this exercise, the hamstrings work strongly – concentrically in raising the weight and eccentrically in lowering it. A partner could provide resistance by holding your foot, allowing it to move more slowly.

Alternatively, kneel as shown in the picture, with weighted leg extended. Curl backwards, bringing the heel towards the behind.

Calf raise or heel raise *(with barbell)*

Muscle groups: foot plantar flexors
Major muscles: gastrocnemius,
soleus

Hold a barbell behind your neck. Rise as high as you can on your toes, maintaining a good balance throughout the movement. Lower slowly. As a progression from this exercise, place a thick board under your toes. Rise on your toes as high as possible and then lower your heels. For maximum effort, do both these exercises with a vigorous push-off.

Dorsal exercises

Most of us work every day with our backs bent forward – we may lean over a desk, work at a table or sit in a car. Consequently the muscles of the back are continually working in a lengthened condition to maintain the body's equilibrium. Systematic strengthening exercises for the back muscles can compensate for this continual stooping and develop a back strong enough to avoid fatigue and strain. The same exercises can be used for those wishing to improve performance in sport or athletics.

The back muscles respond well to training, but it is important, at the risk of being repetitious, to remember this one basic principle: never lift weights with the back bent forward and rounded. It is from such a movement that intervertebral disc trouble springs. The short muscles and ligaments which retain the discs in position are easily damaged when heavy weights are lifted in this rounded-back position. Once this has happened there is always the possibility of recurring trouble. So the importance of keeping the back straight when lifting cannot be over emphasized. The exercises given below work the back muscles either in their normal length or between a normal and a shortened one.

Bent over rowing – single arm *(with dumb-bells)*

Muscle groups: shoulder retractor, back extensors
Major muscles: posterior deltoid, latissimus dorsi, teres major

Select a fairly heavy dumb-bell. Lean forward at the waist, one foot about a pace in front of the other. Place your free hand on the forward knee to support the upper body firmly on the non-working arm. From this starting position bend and stretch the arm to bring the elbow well back as far beyond the shoulder as you can manage. Repeat one side then change over and work the other side, using the same number of reps. As a variation, you can rotate the body slightly in pulling the

dumb-bell back, thus throwing work upon the abdominal oblique muscles.

Another variation would be to support your body by placing your free hand on a bench or chair. Pull the dumb-bell vigorously up to the shoulder.

Trunk bending sideways *(with dumb-bells)*

Muscle groups: back extensors
Major muscles: latissimus dorsi, erector spinae

Stand holding a dumb-bell in each hand, feet astride. Keeping the body erect, bend sideways at the hips to the left and then to the right in a rhythmical movement. Do not use very heavy dumb-bells in this exercise, for the muscular effort involved must not only pull the weight over to the side but check the momentum and gravitational pull so as to change the swing to the opposite direction.

Trunk raising backwards *(without weights)*

Muscle groups: back extensors
Major muscles: sacrospinalis, gluteus maximus

This exercise offers opportunities for progression which will bring in other muscle groups, but if you are a beginner you should practise the simple form of the exercise first. Lie face downwards on the floor, hands clasped behind your back. Try to raise your head and spine as far as possible off the ground – when your back is strong enough you can lift your feet. Tuck the chin well in. You can increase the resistance by raising your arms so that your fingertips touch the side of your head and also by holding a disc weight behind your neck.

Back extension from a bench

Muscle groups: extensors of the back
Major muscle: sacrospinalis

Lie face downwards on a bench, with a partner holding your legs firmly down. Allow your body to hang down over the end of the bench. With hands holding a light disc behind the neck, stretch backwards, extending your spine as fully as possible. Lower your body and repeat.

Chest exercises

Chest exercises are some of the most important of all weight training exercises for women. They develop and strengthen the pectoral muscles of the chest, the triceps, the deltoids and to a secondary extent, the latissimus dorsi, all of which are responsible for an important range of movements – such as pushing an object away from your body or pushing your body away from an object.

The specially selected exercises described below promote deep respiration. The vital capacity of the lungs increases to cope with the additional load thrown upon the respiratory system, and this vastly improves the mobility of the chest walls. This gives a better profile to the rib cage.

Not suprisingly, weight training coaches frequently recommend these chest exercises as being particularly valuable in figure shaping routines, as well as for their benefits for athletes and sportswomen. (*See also* Chapter 11.)

The bench press (i) *(with barbell)*

> *Muscle groups: arm extensors, shoulder flexors*
> *Major muscles: frontal fibres of deltoid, pectorals, triceps*

Always have a trained partner standing by when attempting this exercise with a heavily weighted barbell.

Lie on the bench holding the barbell across your chest, wide overgrasp. Press the weight upwards to stretch height above the shoulders, keeping the arms vertical. If you move your hands closer together more work is done by the triceps and less by the pectorals.

When a heavy barbell is used, take it off the rack (or training partner), lower to the chest and then press it to a straight arm position. Do not bring the barbell down quickly or control might be lost. Take care to breathe correctly.

The bench press (ii) *(with dumb-bells)*

> *Muscle groups: arm extensors*
> *Major muscles: frontal fibres of the deltoid*

The bench press is a little more difficult with dumb-bells; each arm has to control its own load, and consequently the lift is not as stable as when a bar joins the two weights. Lie on the bench with dumb-bells held above the chest. Bend arms so the elbows approach the floor and the dumb-bells are directly above each elbow joint. Stretch your arms upwards and then lower to the start position. Breathe in when pressing upwards and out as you reach the extended position of the arms. With heavy dumb-bells make sure that you have a spotter standing by, in case you get into a situation where you are unable to control the weights – sometimes called 'getting pinned'.

Bent arm sideways raise or dumb-bell flys

Muscle groups: shoulder horizontal flexors
Major muscles: deltoid, pectorals, coracobrachialis

Lie on your back on the bench with your arms sideways and slightly bent at the elbow. Hold the dumb-bells with the thumbs uppermost. Raise the weights to the position above and across the chest and lower slowly down, following the same arc of movement. Breathe in as you bring the weights upwards and breathe out as you lower them slowly to the ground. Keep your arms slightly bent during the whole movement, do not lock them straight at the top position. This is one of the best chest, shoulder and arm exercises.

Straight arm pullover *(with barbell)*

Muscle groups: shoulder extensors
Major muscles: pectorals, teres major, latissimus dorsi, triceps

Lie on your back on the bench with a light barbell held at arm's length overhead. Slowly lower the bar backwards over the head until the weights are close to the floor, still at arm's length behind the head. During the lowering, you will feel your rib-cage 'fanning' out as the weight reaches the last position of the exercise. Raise the bar on the return movement following the same arc and keeping your arms straight and the hips firm on the bench. This is a first-class mobilising and strengthening exercise.

Double bent arm pullover *(with barbell)*

Muscle groups: shoulder extensors, shoulder flexors, thorax, arm extensors
Major muscles: deltoid, pectorals, teres major, latissimus dorsi, triceps

Lie on the bench, feet flat on the floor or on the bench, head supported on the bench. Reach back behind the head then grasp the barbell with an overgrasp, while keeping the elbows bent, pull the barbell up and over the head to rest on the chest. Take the barbell back over the head, keeping it close to the head with the arms bent all the time. Repeat.

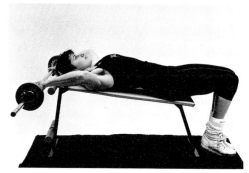

Special care should be taken with all these chest exercises. Do not struggle to exercise with barbells or dumb-bells that are too heavy for you. When a spotter is helping you to replace a barbell on a rack above your head **never let go** yourself until you are sure the barbell is resting firmly on the rack.

You can introduce variety into the exercises by changing the width of grip on the barbell. In a bench press, for example, a wide grip throws more work upon the frontal fibres of the deltoids and the outer fibres of the pectorals. A narrow grip puts more stress upon the triceps and inner fibres of the pectorals. Additionally, the effect of the exercises can be modified by using a bench on an incline or decline. These variations will not only relieve any boredom with the routine, they will also encourage more complete physical development.

CHAPTER SIX   **Exercises on machines**

Exercising on machines has already been mentioned in the Introduction and in Chapter 2. This chapter will look at different exercises on different machines in more detail.

When comparing the use of machines with free weights, there is one subtle difference that you might at first not notice: with most weight training exercises using barbells or dumb-bells, there is often a position at the end of the movement where there is hardly any resistance at all. For example, in the overhead press and the bench press, the squat, arm curls and several other exercises, there is a 'lock-out' point at the end of the movement where the weight can be held without a great deal of effort. It is a point at which the resistance is removed from the muscles and placed upon bones and joints. Consequently muscles can then relax without the weight being dropped and no purposeful exercise is being provided for the muscles at this point. When these same exercises are performed on machines, you have to maintain the muscular effort to hold that end position, thus providing additional and effective resistance for your muscle development.

In addition to the lock-out point there is also a 'sticking point' – a position at which no further movement is possible. It happens, for example, with athletes who can manage a heavy weight in the overhead press; they then find that there is one stage of the movement – usually the begining or the end – in which they just cannot manage the extra poundage. So for part of the movement only part of the muscle is worked heavily, whilst for the rest of the movement inadequate resistance is being provided for optimum muscular development. Exercise machines can provide just that finely graded resistance which works the muscles evenly through their full range of movement.

In other words, what you have to bear in mind in planning your training schedule is that when a muscle contracts, its effective strength changes, as the leverage and the direction of movement upon it changes. Therefore the best exercise for muscle development is one that provides the correct variable resistance uniformly throughout the exercise.

Arm and shoulder exercises

Multi-biceps, arm curls

This new machine has been designed to develop the arm flexor muscles without putting too much stress upon the wrist. Performed in a seated position, the exercise ensures that there is no cheating of the kind which can be done with the barbell curl – by swinging your body backwards at the hips to aid the lift. In this exercise, graded resistance is provided throughout the movement.

The exercise improves the efficiency of the biceps brachialis – the two-headed muscle of the arm – in its function of supinating (turning the palm upwards) the forearm as well as flexing the elbow joint.

Multi-triceps, extension exercise

This exercise develops the triceps – which extend the elbow joint and assist in the adduction (drawing the upper arm in towards the body) of the upper arm – without throwing any strain upon other muscles of the body. For comfort it is done sitting down.

Multi-triceps exercises perfectly complement the muscular activity involved with the multi-biceps work, ensuring harmonious development of the shoulder girdle.

Lateral raise

The smooth, efficient, direct exercise on this machine develops the anterior, middle and posterior fibres of the triangular deltoid which hides the bony prominences of the shoulder joints. This is a very hard-working muscle for although its chief action is the abduction of the arms, from the sides to a horizontal position, its anterior fibres draw the arms forward and bring them up to vertical above the head and the posterior fibres draw the arms backwards. A well-developed deltoid muscle forms a pleasingly rounded and shapely cap to the shoulder joint.

Overhead raise

The deltoid, supraspinatus and triceps are given graduated resistance in all phases of this exercise. Together with the lateral raise, these two exercises offer a superb shoulder girdle work-out.

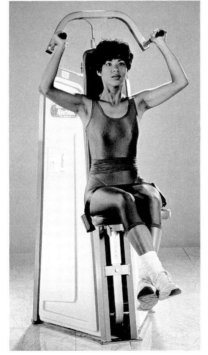

Abdominal exercises

In order to develop the vertical muscles of the abdomen – recti abdominis – you need to use resistance training on those powerful pillars of muscle which originate from the crest of the pubis and are inserted into the cartilages of the fifth, sixth and seventh ribs. These muscles not only act to resist the pressure of weighty abdominal contents but also are most important, along with the oblique abdominal muscles, for the maintenance of good erect posture. They are used in:

- bending the spinal column sideways
- rotating the vertical column
- flexing the vertical column, which is performed mainly by the recti abdominis

The actions of these muscles, which form the anterior abdominal wall, are not in fact separate functions – as has been suggested above for the purpose of description – and therefore the exercises recommended for them takes into consideration the fact that they work in support of one another in most of the natural movements of the body.

The two machine exercises described and illustrated here – the mid-torso curl and the rotary torso – provide a reliable method for improving the figure as well as generally strengthening the abdominal wall.

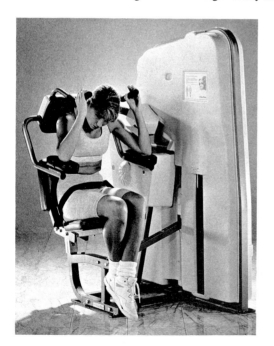

The mid-torso curl

This is a new machine which provides correct and variable resistance for the abdominal muscles, especially to those which flex the waist. The machine is so structured to cater for abdominal muscle isolation and torso stability and is therefore excellent for developing your stomach muscles and improving your silhouette.

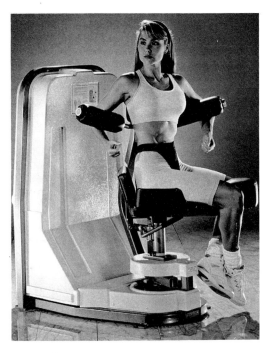

The rotary torso

This machine has been specially designed to provide resistance exercise for the internal and external oblique muscles of the abdomen. When you work on the new rotary torso machine you will experience the feeling of exercising your oblique muscles for a specific, rotational function.

Strengthening the oblique muscles is essential for turning and twisting. Additionally, the obliques are important for the containment and protection of the abdominal organs, which have a tendency to slump forward, resting heavily against the abdominal wall.

Hip exercises

The hip joints perform complex movements which are controlled by several muscle groups. If you are training for sport, athletics or figure development you need to know how all these muscles act together in various combinations.

Here are the main combinations:
- Flexion of the hip – uses the rectus femoris (quadriceps), psoas, iliacus, sartorius and adductors.
- Extension of the hip – uses the gluteus maximus, biceps femoris (hamstrings), semimembranosus, semitendinosus, and the fibres of the adductor magnus.
- Abduction of the hip – uses the gluteus medius, gluteus minimus, sartorius and tensor fasciae latae.
- External rotation of the hip – uses the small muscles arising from the hip bone and inserted into the back of the upper end of the femur, also the sartorius.
- Internal rotation of the hip – uses the gluteus medius, gluteus minimus, sartorius tensor fasciae latae, and psoas major.

Individual exercises can be done to work the muscle groups and strengthen their range of movement for each action.

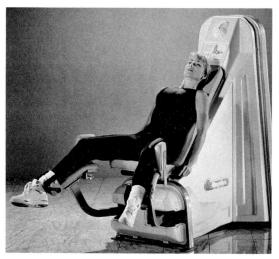

Hip abduction

This machine trains the muscles of the outer thighs, firming and strengthening them. These are the muscles which move the legs outwards. The hip abduction machine offers a precise and controlled resistance to the gluteus media muscles as the legs stretched outwards in a steady, deliberate manner.

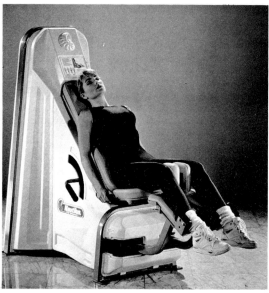

Hip adduction

The muscles of the inner thighs are worked strongly in this exercise. Easily controlled levers allow you to control the resistance being offered to the working muscles.

Both these exercise machines provide thorough exercise for the muscles which allow you to stop, turn, change direction and accelerate suddenly.

Leg exercises

After you have completed the hip exercises it is a logical progression to work on your legs. In order to achieve a balanced schedule of exercises for the lower limbs the following exercises are recommended.

Seated leg curl

The hamstring muscles, occupying the outer portion of the back of the thighs, are powerful flexors of the knee joints and also play an important part in maintaining a graceful erect posture. These are the muscles which lift the body upwards, as in rising from a stooping position. Strength exercises for these muscles can be most beneficial.

You will need to adjust the machine to find the correct exercise position for you and to adjust the resistance offered to suit your build and physical development. It is especially important that you are not too ambitious and are careful to avoid injury.

Prone leg curl

As in the previous exercise, the hamstrings are exercised through a full range of movement.

Leg extension

Strong quadriceps muscles – a four-headed muscle occupying most of the front of each thigh – are not only important for posture and for extending your knees but for stabilising the knee joints – the most unstable joints in the whole body. The main support for the knees comes from ligaments and the quadriceps and the whole is vulnerable to injury.

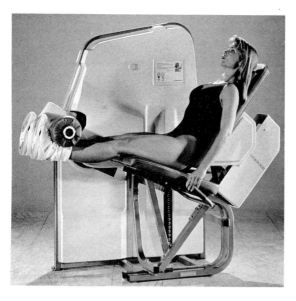

If the the muscles of the front of your thigh are weak through lack of use or injury, then the ligaments of the knee joint are put under considerable strain. Thigh muscles waste away very quickly after a severe knee injury. The best way to protect your knees is to keep your muscles strong. The repair of damaged knee joints and muscles can take several weeks of healing and careful exercise.

The leg extension machine is an ideal way of strengthening your quadriceps muscles. But remember, when you are working on this machine you must make sure that your knee stays absolutely straight and remains straight at the end of each movement before bending again. You will be wasting your time if you do the exercise with your knees even slightly bent at the end of the extension movement.

Seated calf

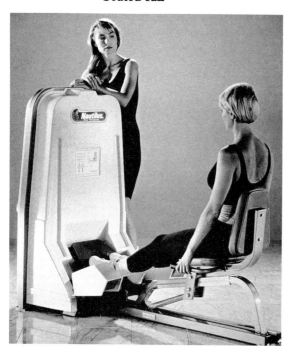

The Nautilus machine is the first to offer an accurate, rotary variable exercise for the belly-shaped calf muscles – gastrocnemius and soleus – situated at the back of the lower leg. The tendons of these two muscles blend into one to form the well-known Achilles tendon, which is attached to the back of the heel bone. They are known as the plantar flexor muscles, which need to be powerful in order to propel you forwards in walking and jumping or simply in raising your body onto your toes.

With this machine the user sits in the ideal position for maximum pre-stretch and contraction of the calf muscles. Remember to extend the ankle as far as possible at the end of each movement.

Dorsal exercises

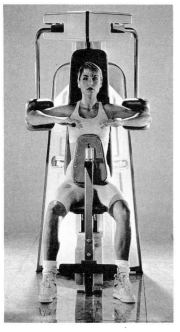

Rowing back

Here is an ideal machine for providing a thorough work-out for the deltoid, rhomboids and trapezius. The rhomboids, lying between the shoulder blade and the spine, and the broad, flat, triangular trapezius – which is attached to the back of the skull, and the upper back – are most important in controlling the movement of the neck, shoulders and spine. They need plenty of purposeful exercise to counter their habitual misuse in day-to-day work. Exercise on this machine is most useful for rehabilitating weakened postural muscles and for developing the strength and endurance needed for the avoidance of round shoulders and 'dowagers' hump'.

Torso arm

By just looking at the photograph of this torso arm machine you could easily get the impression that this is yet another arm exercise. In fact, most of the muscular effort in pulling down the bars is being done by the broadest muscle of the back – the latissimus dorsi. The latissimus dorsi is another large triangular muscle which covers the lumbar and lower half of the thoracic region. Its fibres are directed upward and outward and converge towards the armpit, and its main action is to bring the arm from an abducted position to the side of the body. But in its reverse action it can pull the body up to the arm; it is also an extensor of the upper arm.

This torso arm machine will work on multiple joints and muscles, offering them effective resistance. The result will be a strengthened back and arms.

The compound row

Uppermost in the minds of the designer of these Nautilus machines for women is the need to provide exercise for the harmonious development of the body. It cannot be emphasized too much how important it is for your muscular development to be balanced. The compound row ensures adequate development of the dorsal muscles to balance those strengthened with the chest work-out machines.

Because the machine eliminates stress on the lower back, injury is highly unlikely. From this point of view it is safer to use than free weights. Even so, exercise with care and do not work against a resistance which puts too much strain on your dorsal muscles.

Chest exercises

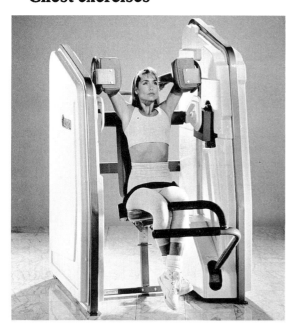

The women's pullover

This machine was specially manufactured in response to the ever-increasing use of machines by women. It provides rotary work for the dorsal muscles – the latissimus dorsi – and for the triceps.

The women's double chest

The pectoral muscles are the broad triangular muscles of the chest which stretch from the sternum and the cartilages of the upper six ribs to the top of the humerus, by the armpit. When the pectoral muscles contract they draw the arms towards the body and can also rotate the upper arm.

The chest machine is particularly

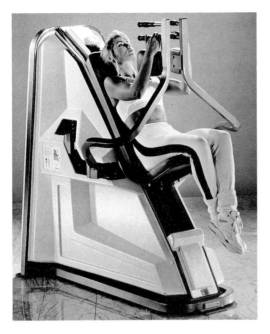

useful because it enhances the stretching of the pectorals at the beginning of the exercise and allows for a total range of movement and complete pectoral contraction at the end of the exercise.

It is often better for muscles to work from a position in which they are fully stretched to the position in which they are fully contracted. Obviously, under ordinary circumstances muscles are rarely required to work through the full range, but on occasion they may have to do so. Active full-range exercises are recognised as beneficial by the medical profession because they maintain joint mobility, increase circulation and ensure an emergency reserve of power and mobility. (*See also* Chapter 11.)

Your training programme on exercise machines

Please remember that exercise machines have been designed to ensure harmonious development of your muscular system. Follow a balanced schedule, taking advantage of the range of machines available. Remember that a weakness in any group of your muscles not only results in diminished stability or some loss of movement from the joint, but creates a state of muscular imbalance which affects all of the groups concerned in the production of coordinated movement. Do make sure that you use the machines to exercise all the muscle groups of your body.

Finally, bear in mind that your drive for fitness or figure development never demands that you push yourself to exhaustion. Enjoy your time in the leisure centre and you will get tremendous rewards for your efforts.

CHAPTER SEVEN   # Weight training for sport

Until the 1970s, weight training was often thought to be unsuitable for the training schedules of some women's sports on the grounds that it would make players' muscles tight and restrict their ability to stretch and jump. Ideas changed when players like nine-times Wimbledon Champion Martina Navratilova were seen using weights in their pre-season conditioning routines.

It is generally agreed that whatever the particular physical capability needed, special training is necessary to develop it in addition to playing and competing regularly. Many dedicated and determined sports-women compete at the highest levels in all avenues of sport – even the martial arts. Their success has been achieved by the same means as sportsmen: by paying careful attention to increasing their fitness and strength and developing a high degree of skill.

If you play at competition level you will find that careful physical conditioning and specific skills are imperative; poor conditioning can be costly, especially in a long and gruelling match. Whether you are a beginner or a more experienced sportswoman, your success depends upon your having more than a good measure of the the six S factors of fitness. They are: skill, stamina, strength, speed, suppleness, spirit.

The six essential attributes of a champion

In the normal course of play the need for great strength, stamina, speed and suppleness arises only on occasion – but such an occasion may become a great sporting moment that goes down in history. So your training programme for improving your performance must include the most effective methods for the development of these special aspects of fitness, using progressive schedules and the overloading of your muscle groups.

When planning your training a balance has to be struck so that you are not spending so much time on physical conditioning that little time is left for actually practising your chosen sport. It will help your decision-making if we take a detailed look at those factors and see how important they are.

Skill

Skill can be developed by coaching, by long hours of purposeful and supervised practice, by watching champions perform, by dedication, concentration, and competition with others. True, there are some people who seem to have a natural bent for ball games or an innate ability for running, but there does come a time when further improvement requires training.

In fact, every basic skill has to be learnt until it can be done automatically, without conscious effort. To a young child it is a natural process and parents talk of these fundamental activities as skills which the child has learnt: the child matures and skills are developed. We recognise skill in other people: we talk about skilled craftswomen, skilful hockey players, and the skill of the surgeon. It means the ability to achieve a high standard of performance consistently.

Sportswomen have found that their skill can be improved, but it has to be learnt until, by practice, they begin to 'feel' the movement so precisely that they know immediately whether their performance is good or bad. A point to note is that certain skills can be lost or impaired when conscious thought is given to them. Witness the player who has lost confidence and tries too hard – she often makes a bigger mess of her game than ever, because by thinking about a stroke she is interfering with an ingrained reflex pattern.

Physiologists explain this by saying that the start of a movement of any skill is controlled by conscious thought in the pre-motor area of the cerebrum, but with practice the coordination is taken over, as a reflex movement, by another part of the brain – the cerebellum. Any adjustments needed to compensate for changing circumstances in a game – such as the distance of a golf ball from the hole, the hockey ball from the goal, the speed of a pass or the position of a tackling defender – are also catered for by reflex adjustments initiated by the cerebellum. Ultimately, with continued practice in actual match conditions, judgement and anticipation improve to such an extent that very little conscious effort is needed.

You must have muscular and cardio-vascular endurance to apply skilful movement throughout the game so that fatigue does not spoil your performance. When muscles are fatigued they send out signals of pain and discomfort; errors are made, accuracy is lost and a greater conscious effort is needed to execute strokes, which at the beginning of play would have been done easily. A higher level of muscular strength and stamina invariably produces a higher and more consistent level of skill. Time must be spent not only in mastering techniques but also in acquiring the muscular ability to use your skills under the stress of top-class competition – when you are physically and mentally tired.

Stamina

Stamina is needed for those long games, perhaps lengthened through the playing of extra time or tie breaks or simply because individuals are evenly matched and the competition is tough. In such cases you might be demanding a wide range of movement from your body such as running, hopping, side-stepping, skipping backwards to the base line, twisting, lunging and hitting with all your power for anything between one and three hours. And throughout this time you must never give your opponent any indication that you are flagging physically. A player who sees a weary opponent immediately gains a psychological advantage. She will become more confident, more patient, knowing she can wait for just the right moment to make a decisive move or shot. Whereas if you feel that you have more staying power than your opponent you have no need to go for the risky strokes played in panic. You can take your time until the opportunity to strike arises when your opponent is out of position. And it is stamina that enables you to push yourself a fraction further than your opponent. It wins matches.

We must be clear about what is meant by the term 'stamina', for there are two kinds of stamina: local muscular and cardio-vascular. Neither of these two qualities can be developed optimally by merely playing the game. Special training schedules are needed such as those described in Chapter 8.

Strength

Strength applied with speed produces power. And power is needed for top class performance in most sports. For example, when a tennis player turns suddenly and dashes to the opposite side of the court she is changing the direction of a projectile weighing perhaps a hundred pounds or more – her body. Precise, fast movement is clearly an asset which enables a skilful player to retrieve balls which a weaker player might leave as unplayable. Similarly, power is needed to lob a squash ball into the corner of the court or smash a shuttlecock hard at the feet of your opponent. You need strength to grip your racket or hockey stick firmly so that power is not dissipated when playing your best shot.

Naturally, some sports require greater strength than others. The swimmer or canoeist has to overcome strong external forces such as the resistance of the body through the water, or the flat blade of the paddle against the water. The external forces to be overcome in some sports clearly will call for additional strength and stamina. Other sports require great flexibility and agility rather than strength, but power for explosive movements could still be important and is useful to have.

The mere practice of your chosen sport will not develop your physical and psychological characteristics to a high enough degree if you want to reach the top. For example, the basketball shooter or volleyball striker who can out-jump opponents has a tremendous advantage, but occasions for jumping high do not happen frequently enough during a game for the player to develop the necessary leg power and coordination required. Nor would actual practice in jumping develop sufficient leg power to make any real improvement in their jumping height. Their skill in jumping would improve and so add a little more height, but the most marked improvement would be seen after strength in the leg extensor muscle had been developed through special resistance exercise.

Strength is the key to success in many sports and it is said that 'a bad strong 'un will always beat a good weak 'un'. But you can plan your training better once you identify how much strength you need to have, of what kind, and then how much time to spend on developing it to be a winner.

Strength for stability

To make any perfect and powerful stroke you need a stable posture. Particularly important for this are the muscles of the back, neck and abdomen, which stabilise the body through a variety of actions while the principal efforts of hitting, throwing and jumping are made by other muscle groups.

Look at it this way: the golfer controls conditions for her stroke: she has as much time as she wants to adjust her stance, consider her swing and her stroke will affect all the factors which determine the direction, flight and speed she imparts to the ball. Yet despite the opportunity for making preparations, unwanted body movements still occur – particularly with the beginner or weaker player – which impair the shot. This is because of involuntary actions of the neuro-muscular system brought about by the stimulation of the muscles making the stroke. How much more likely are such distracting movements to occur in games which require rapid reaction to a ball or shuttlecock moving in a wide variety of directions and at different speeds?

The body uses a high degree of skill to coordinate muscles, and strength is required to fix it in flight or to adopt a stretched position from which winning shots are played. You may be hitting a featherweight shuttlecock, but your back and shoulders are supporting a head and trunk which depend on them for stability. To make a winning stroke your body must be in the best possible position to channel the power being driven into the stroke. And it must be in position before the striking action is begun. This is accomplished by good footwork and by having the body firmly stabilised by strong, well-developed muscles. Strong muscles respond well to reflex stimuli and make moves and shots possible which weaker players fail to achieve mainly because the body is in a disadvantaged position from the start.

The position of the head determines the way your body moves in flight. If a cat is dropped upside down, the first movement it makes is with its head, all other body movements follow to ensure a safe landing position – on its feet. Similarly divers, gymnasts and free-fall parachutists learn how movement of the head and limbs alters the body position in flight, and good stability as well as agility will help them.

The pull of gravity has, naturally, to be given consideration. For example, little effort is needed to turn the head and torso backwards when standing but much more muscular strength is needed to do the same movement when the torso is stretched forward – as might happen in a dive across a tennis court.

The more that muscle action is analysed the more obvious becomes the need for all-round strength. Even with sports which may appear less vigorous, increased strength will often improve performance. Take rifle shooting for example; muscular strength leads to better scores because the arms can be held steady while aim is being taken.

Triathletes find enormous strength and stamina is essential. Competitions are very long and tiring; those who can overcome the distractions of fatigue are more able to maintain perfect coordination and consistency for the extra critical minutes which might make all the difference between winning and being runner-up. Obviously championship form demands more than just all-round fitness; as so many international competitors have found, you need a reserve – just that little bit extra – so that you never give up. In this way you can turn a result around and take the initiative.

Speed

Quickness off the mark is an attribute of many successful sportswomen. Agile players move so rapidly backwards and sideways, as well as forwards, always on balance, poised to react quickly to an opponent's moves. Drive comes from the knees and ankles. They do not stand flat footed but are always ready, bouncing on their toes so that body inertia does not have to be overcome; their knees are slightly flexed and powerful leg muscles ready to make short driving steps to get off the mark and change direction quickly. Being able to sprint across a court or within a limited area of a pitch marks the difference between a star and the average club player. It is an ability developed through special training, not just by playing.

The key to having speed often lies in good anticipation, reading the game, keeping alert, having responsive reflexes. These skills demand explosive power and we have already seen that the basic ingredient of this is strength. Off-season training with weights will develop that strength needed for powerful acceleration, especially when your weight training schedule is combined with activities such as shuttle-running, turning and twisting and sprinting over fifteen to twenty yards; if you are lucky a coach will help you by giving commands to change direction, which – literally – keeps you on your toes.

Strength and stamina training will give you power, and if you use your strength and aggression as a positive force in situations where you need a quick defence, you will have that marvellous feeling of saying to yourself, 'Take that!' as you drive a hockey ball into the back of the net or crunch down a smash into your opponent's court.

Suppleness

Suppleness is the ability to flex and extend and to increase your range of movement. It enables you to have better balance so that you can conserve energy by lithesome, apparently effortless movements.

Gymnasts and dancers have long recognised the fact that stretching exercises are most beneficial to performance. Even macho soccer players and boxers have submitted to ballet exercises because they know it helps to improve their game. By the same token, it is well known that limited flexibility results in restricted movement, which can adversely affect performance. Furthermore, just as muscles deteriorate with disuse, losing their strength and size, so do joints; they stiffen up, mobility is lost and this limits the range of movements that a player can make.

Some sports, such as diving, gymnastics and the martial arts, demand a very high degree of flexibility and agility, whilst others do not require quite as much. Nevertheless the flexibility needed for a particular sport can best be developed by specific routines designed to stretch muscles and work joints through a full range of movement. The experience of doctors who specialise in sports injuries is that increased flexibility guards against injury. Flexible players are less prone to strains and tears of muscles and tendons. For example, 60 per cent of basketball injuries which put players out of action were found to be the result of improper conditioning. Mobilising exercises should therefore form an essential part of pre-season training and continue to be performed during the season itself. This does not mean that you should aim for hyper-flexibility, pushing your joints beyond their natural limits; there is little to be gained from it, indeed it can be dangerous.

Spirit

Playing is fun but winning is more fun. It was once an accepted British tradition that we play games for fun and try to win for the game itself rather than for any tangible reward. But now the rewards are more tempting and winning has become more worthwhile.

In most avenues of sport competition is tough and getting to the top is hard work. Those who excel often do so because they devote more and more time to training. Most of us have a wide variety of demands upon our time – study, work and social activities. It is important that any time spent in training should be used as efficiently as possible in order to achieve a high standard in all the elements of skill, stamina, strength, speed and suppleness – the essential components of good performance.

There is no easy route to the top; any champion will tell you there are no short cuts. Those who do achieve the rewards and honours of a successful sporting career do so because they have that elusive but vital element of spirit – the final S factor mentioned at the beginning of this chapter. They have the spirit which is a characteristic of every champion: it is the 'will to win'. Naturally, most sportspeople want to win, and the competitive spirit is inherent in most of us, but few have the dedication and the determination to make the sacrifices of time and money to pour every ounce of effort into their game and develop an intense will to win that overcomes all difficulties and setbacks. This spirited determination is not just something people are born with; the tenacity and mental power that can drive the body to greater feats can be developed in the same way as the other S factors. It all depends upon where the motivation comes from that makes sports players want to be the very best. Some people have an inner compulsion to fight hard for success, stemming from a desire for fame or fortune or simply 'to show them' – whoever 'they' might be. It is not too difficult to manufacture your own motivation, to set yourself goals and give yourself credible reasons for achieving them. Once the motivation is established then the determination to succeed inevitably follows. It is this determination that can tip the balance one way or the other in an even match.

Whether your personal goal is to win the club championship, the national or the world championship, there is much to be learnt from studying how the champions themselves found their motivation or way to win. Read their biographies; if you are lucky enough to meet them, pick their brains, learn from their experience and you will eventually come to the conclusion that the way we think determines what we are and what we can be. It is something borne out by the experience of winners in all walks of life – that if you want something and go for it determinedly you will be astonished at what you can achieve.

Training to win

It might seem, in some sports, that champions and players selected for international teams get younger every year, but close analysis usually reveals that these youngsters have come a long way since they first took up the sport, and their training has been carefully phased. We can all learn from their progress and achievements.

No matter what stage you are at in your sporting career your training should still be phased to give maximum benefits. There are usually three major phases with some overlapping of course. They are: pre-season, in-season and off- or post-season.

One of the advantages of phasing training programmes into three separate stages is that recognisable targets can be set and achieved within certain periods of time, gradually leading up to the week when a peak of fitness and performance is required. Each sport obviously has its own particular balance of the basic S factors and this would be taken into consideration by you and your coach. When planning your complete programme, bear in mind individual differences in physique – your programme may be different to that of your friends. It is a waste of valuable time if you are practising a technique which is too difficult for your muscles to perform correctly. Inadequate strength and insufficient powers of endurance are the fundamental causes of poor style. Your post-season and pre-season conditioning programme should rectify this deficiency. Let's look briefly at those three phases of training.

Phase one: pre-season

This is an in between time, a period following the post-season rest and subsequent training when the heart and lungs have been thoroughly exercised in the variety of ways explained later in this chapter. And it is a time when weight training can still be employed advantageously for improving strength and power whilst still maintaining cardio-vascular fitness. It is also a transitional phase because during the latter stages, more time can be devoted to practising your skills and tactical moves in the game. As the competitive season draws near, the individual's work load is eased to allow the body to adjust to the demands made by competing.

Phase two: in-season

All too often inadequate strength and insufficient stamina have been blamed for poor results. But with careful training you can be in much better shape than ever before by the time the competitive season arrives. In phase two much less time is available for weight training; tactical moves and skill practice must take precedence, dominating the schedule absolutely. Nevertheless (especially if you are in athletics), you may still feel the need for one or two short sessions of weight training each week. It is a matter of individual choice; women who weight train in the playing season say it helps to maintain their strength and flexibility gained through the more concentrated weight training sessions of the earlier phases.

Obviously, it is not possible to be state categorically fixed timetables for the phases of training; with the recent boom of indoor tournaments some sports are in season all year round. There will also be differences in circumstances of those wishing to train. Though there is much to be said for team members training together, this is not always possible, especially for amateur teams whose members often have conflicting commitments. This is especially so with women's teams where members often hold two jobs – one outside the home and one within! They have to fit in their training as and when it is most convenient for them to do so. However, if this sounds like you, don't worry, you can still plan your year's conditioning programme in a way that will allow you to benefit from the three-phase approach.

Phase three: post-season

It takes about forty-eight hours for athletes and sports players to recover from a heavy work out, but there comes a time when, after a gruelling season, a longer period of rest and recuperation is advisable. Most people find that a complete break away from training and competition for a week or two helps them to return to a hard schedule better.

The weeks after this physiological and psychological rest period is are a time for tough weight training and stamina training schedules which can improve strength and stamina without interfering with performance in the competitive season. Time can also be spent in strengthening muscles supporting joints which are subject to great strain from sudden turns and twists. Ankles and knee joints in particular are susceptible to early season injuries and the off-season is an ideal opportunity for preventive training.

An important aim for this training period should be the development of cardio-vascular fitness. Running, cycling and circuit training with weights could well take up a major part of the off-season training time.

Training for stamina

We saw earlier in this chapter that there are two forms of stamina: local muscular and cardio-vascular. Furthermore, the qualities which enable a hockey player to dash, turn, twist and flick-in a hard shot are very different from the qualities of the 5000-metre runner. Training for long-distance running, for example, much of which consists of cross-country running or doing numerous laps of a track, develops a sense of rhythm which enables the runner to maintain the same speed with a minimum expenditure of energy. Cultivating this style of running and stamina is not of much use to the hockey player as the stresses of the game demand alertness and the physical capacity for repeated bouts of sprinting and turning. The stamina of the hockey player, and indeed for other such types of sport, depends largely upon your ability to relax and recuperate between intensive efforts, and upon the elasticity and sensitivity of your tissues. In most games you must be balanced so that you are able to swiftly glide through a range of coordinated movements.

If you rely mainly on long-distance running for developing stamina, you will develop cardio-vascular endurance but not that particular kind of stamina which allows you to be active without becoming weary. For these reasons coaches are more concerned with specific endurance training for particular sports. For example, in tennis, players train by placing six balls on one side of the service line towards the net, another six on the other side of the line some distance away and six more in a group at the net. Each group of balls is given a number, 'one', 'two' and 'three'. Then a training partner will stand behind the trainee who stands at the centre of the baseline. She will shout a number, for instance, 'one' and the player has to dash forward at full speed, pick up a ball from the group and then dash backwards and place it on the baseline. When 'three' is shouted the player then sprints to the net, picks up a ball and again runs backwards to the baseline. And so the routine goes on without pause until all eighteen balls have been collected. In other words, the player is moving about rapidly under pressure, as if reaching shots, short and long, from an opponent. The important thing to note about this type of endurance training is that they never know just what the next call will be. It calls for balance and concentration with agility and readiness to move in any direction and back again – as you would in a game – without any time for a breather in between.

This kind of special training develops local muscular endurance at the same time as general cardio-vascular. Weight training exercises can develop endurance in the muscles which are in particular need of this quality. Thus through specific endurance training, specific physiological changes take place within the muscles concerned. They become more efficient at oxidising both glucose and fat completely. As a result of this, there is less lactic acid build-up, which means that endurance time is prolonged and the onset of fatigue delayed. In addition to these changes, there are those of the circulatory system: muscles which have been through a stamina training routine for some time open up more capillaries which allows energy fuel and oxygen to be more readily available and also facilitates the elimination of the waste products from the increased activity.

The heart muscle responds to endurance training in the same way as the skeletal muscles, by becoming bigger and stronger. Hypertrophy, as this growth is called, is a natural and beneficial development which enables the heart to pump a greater volume of blood into the arteries with each beat: its stroke volume is raised. This cardiac hypertrophy, or 'athlete's heart' is very common and illustrates the principle of specific training, i.e. the heart develops to cope with the increased demand placed upon it by the the body. On average, increases in heart volume in athletes over sedentary individuals is in the region of 25 per cent. At one time medical opinion believed that an enlarged heart in athletes would lead to premature death. Nowadays it is universally recognised that the hypertrophy of sports players' hearts leads not merely to improved performance but also to better health and the likelihood of living longer.

It is because of the increased efficiency of the heart in pumping more blood into the arteries with each beat that the heart rate of the trained athlete drops considerably, sometimes into the lower forties, whilst that of the untrained though healthy woman would be in the region of sixty to seventy beats a minute.

Not only does the heart and thus the circulatory system improve when muscles have been worked to their limits in a rigorous training programme, but the respiratory system also shows marked improvement. Controlled scientific experiments have shown that for the performance of the same amount of work an athlete who has undergone stamina-type training with and without weights takes in a smaller volume of air than the non-athlete. This seems to indicate that stamina training develops a more efficient system for the oxygenation of blood. More oxygen is absorbed from a given volume of air.

Finally, there is one more benefit to be considered. By its very nature stamina training can be physically hard and often the mind has to push the body just that little further than comfort would like. To do this it has to disregard the alarm signals flashing from tired muscles wanting to rest. Eventually the mind becomes accustomed to rejecting these signals, the distress symptoms fade, and the body, which always errs on the safe side of its limits, forges ahead to greater feats still. This is why the mountaineer can force a way through driving snow and blasting winds to conquer the peaks and the tennis champion keeps hammering away because her mind knows that she can make additional demands upon her body even though her lungs feel fit to burst and her heart is pounding in her ears! Being aware of your stamina threshold will give you confidence when the going gets tough.

Now let us look at specific stamina training schedules for the sports woman and in particular circuit training. A word of caution will not come amiss here. Stamina training should be vigorous; train hard and with a regular schedule, but do not overtrain. When you are not in competition you do not need to demand the limit from yourself. Be sensible and remember to have a quota of lighter training days. Do not be tempted to push yourself too far simply because you are feeling so much fitter. This indeed is something you have to guard against, because as your training schedule progresses it becomes easier, your muscles get stronger, your cardio-vascular system increases in capacity, your body becomes more flexible and you will be experiencing that 'high' sensation that is a feeling of euphoria after exercise. This is the time to keep your ambitions in check. Let your training continue to be steady and comfortably progressive.

Don't compare yourself with others in the gym. All that matters is the progress made from your starting point of a few weeks earlier. The important thing now is to keep going. Make sure your week is so organised that it can accommodate your weight training sessions. Get into the habit of completing a progress chart showing personal weight, waist or thigh measurements, heart rate, the number of repetitions that you have achieved and the poundage that you are training with. Charts can be great motivators. They show you the goals already achieved and targets for sessions to come.

Be prepared for some modifications to your routine. Whilst a regular routine is always preferable, it would be unrealistic not to expect the need for occasional modifications.

Circuit training

The circuit or sequence system of weight training, mentioned in Chapter 4, is generally regarded as one of the most effective forms of stamina training. The exercises selected involve systematic hard work for all the major muscle groups of the body, such as the arm flexors, arm extensors, dorsal, abdominal and chest groups, and a special bias towards those big muscle groups situated in the legs and hips – the gluteus maximus in particular.

You need not, of course, depend entirely upon your weight training routines for developing your stamina and general fitness. Consider also taking physical recreation in other ways such as swimming, cycling and brisk walking. No two individuals are alike in their needs for physical development or rehabilitation following a long period of inactivity or sickness. And in recognising these different needs we can adapt conditioning programmes to provide a very personal and enjoyable schedule, which could well be a combination of weight training and other activities. Remember the old saying: Variety is the spice of life.

Other activities

Cycling is a quick way of taking exercise that tones up the whole body and when taken at a businesslike pace it burns up excess fat at the rate of 700 calories an hour. The heart, lungs and circulatory system have to work hard but without any strain being thrown upon joints of the knee, ankle and hip joints. The bike bears the weight and the muscles provide the power. And one of the bonuses of cycling is that you can supplement your weight training routine by cycling to work and to the gym. Like the advice given to weight trainers, though, there are no prizes for forcing yourself to the limits of your endurance. Progress in the same way as you would with weight training, steadily increasing the pace and the degree of difficulty and you will have an excellent complement to your regular sessions with weights.

Swimming too is often recommended as a complement to a weight training routine. The variety it brings into your training makes keeping fit all the more enjoyable. Swimming develops every muscle group of the body harmoniously and is of tremendous value for those who might be recovering from injuries or nerve damage, for the body's weight is partially supported by water, thus sparing sensitive areas, swollen joints or weakened muscles. Once you are feeling fitter you could well feel like tackling other activities.

Which ever activity you choose as a supplement to your weight training programme, do bear in mind that healthy fatigue is far better than sheer exhaustion. It is all very well to be inspired to greater efforts because of the improvement that your weight training has brought but too much can do more harm than good. Take it steadily along with your weight training and you will soon experience the exhilaration of being really fit.

Circuit training can be very strenuous. You may want to start with some of the more difficult exercises. And you might be able to cope with a tough schedule. To avoid this temptation, take it easy and warm-up well before starting the circuit. Simple warming-up and stretching exercises are described in Chapter 3.

The circuit training card shown here shows how you can record exercise by exercise the maximum number of repetitions you have managed to achieve at each session compared to the target you would like to reach.

CIRCUIT TRAINING CARD

Date training begins: _____
Weight of trainee: _____

Exercises	Max Reps	Trg Task	Max Reps	Trg Task
1　Trunk curls 2　Step-ups 3　Arm curls 4　Trunk raising backwards 5　Bench press 6　Half squat				

Dates of Testing: _____

The circuit suggested on the training card is designed to allow you to start training at a safe level of exertion and to progress to harder work as soon as you are fit enough to do so. (*See also* Chapter 4.) When two laps of the circuit can be completed comfortably, new exercises should be introduced one at a time. Test yourself every two weeks; keep a note of the number of repetitions that you complete. Those that can be done more than thirty times, maximum, in your two-week test should be replaced by more difficult exercises, or made more demanding by adding extra resistance.

Circuit training provides a positive stimulus to further effort because you see the improvements and, because progress can be measured, you have a clear idea of what you wish to achieve and know that you will achieve it. The gratification that comes with noting all this progress boosts your motivation to continue, and the circle continues. You set yourself further targets to aim at and get even more satisfaction from achieving them.

> It is generally agreed that:
>
> - Weight training, either with free weights or machines, does not interfere with patterns of complex skills needed for top class performance in sport.
> - The outstanding players will be those who have the strength and stamina skill and experience, to deal with situations and exploit opportunities as they arise.

Specificity of training should be considered when planning the whole conditioning programme. The next chapter looks at the specific needs of some of those sports.

CHAPTER EIGHT

Weight training schedules for major sports

This chapter provides the sportswoman with weight training guidance for most of the major sports so that individuals can compare similarities between sporting activities and prepare programmes to suit their own particular needs. There is, without doubt, something to be gained from considering the requirements of sports other than your own.

Everyone knows that different sports require differing skills and levels of stamina, both general and specific. Sometimes it is convenient to classify sports into categories according to the skills which are required for that activity; but such broad classifications are too general for our purposes. For simplicity of presentation, the suggested weight training schedules recommended for each sport have been listed from the exercises in Chapter 5 with free weights, but the equivalent exercises on machines (in Chapter 6) are equally recommended. Throughout this section of the book, specificity of training has been emphasised, but in the end it will be the individual sportswoman who will discover which combination of training methods produce the best results. Then your training schedules can be adjusted accordingly. Try a few combinations first.

One final word. The key to success with every training programme is 'organisation'. Plan your programme so that other activities do not interfere with your training time. Write down what you plan to do and record your achievements, then you can readily see what is still to be done.

Here are the specific weight training schedules presented in such a way that both the beginner and the more advanced sportswoman can plan from them.

Archery

All-round strength for postural stability is definitely needed for archery. A firm base is essential for stability, which aids accuracy; as the bow is drawn back to its anchor point where the pulling arm rests at full draw, your whole body has to hold steady. A muscle weakness produces shakiness. Weight training exercises for the whole body will ensure a stable posture to aid your position; specific exercises for the upper back, neck and shoulder girdle will provide a full training programme.

A suggested weight training routine would be:

> 1 Warm-up and stretching exercises
> 2 Bench press (chest exercise, p.56)
> 3 Press behind the neck (arm exercise, p.43)
> 4 Trunk curl (abdominal exercise, p.45)
> 5 Trunk raising backwards (dorsal exercise, p.54)
> 6 Wrist curl (arm exercise, p.40)
> 7 Triceps extension (arm exercise, p.42)

Badminton

To improve your game of badminton you should consider the importance of all the S factors mentioned in Chapter 7. In particular, you need to be very supple.

Work on your cardio-vascular efficiency in your pre-season conditioning programme. Usually coaches advise players to run steadily round a track or across an open field, but to break the run with short bursts of 30-metre sprinting, running backwards, zig-zag running and diagonal running backwards.

Specific weight training exercises such as those set out below will improve your power and local muscular endurance. These are for the skills you will be needing in a closely contested match. Work on these during your in-season training. To develop your strength and stamina, circuit training is recommended. You can have an ongoing programme through all three stages.

A suggested weight training routine would be:

> 1 Warming-up and stretching and sprinting across the court
> 2 Trunk curls with twist (abdominal exercise, p.46)
> 3 Bench press (chest exercise, p.56)
> 4 Arm curls (arm exercise, p.38)
> 5 Trunk raising backwards (dorsal exercise, p.54)
> 6 Trunk twisting and lowering backwards (abdominal exercise, p.46)
> 7 Squat jumps (leg exercise, p.47)
> 8 Wrist curls (arm exercise, p.40)
> 9 Triceps extension (arm exercise, p.42)

In addition to the three-phase conditioning programme, badminton coaches often recommend a pre-match warming up routine of heel raising, arm circling, side bending, trunk circling with hamstring stretching, side and forward lunges to stretch the abductor and adductor muscles of the thighs, and a final short sprint to raise the heart rate ready for the game.

Basketball

Women's basketball has become increasingly popular since making its debut in the Olympic Games of 1976. It demands a high level of fitness and agility. Without doubt, basketball can be described as a running and power game. Clearly, cardio-vascular endurance is needed for those wishing to play at league level. Strength is needed in many parts of the body, for which specific weight training exercises are recommended.

For a rebounder, powerful, strong legs are essential, as are well-developed arms and shoulders. The weight training exercises listed below will cater for this aspect of physical conditioning. In addition the rebounding skill of jumping up and down, touching the backboard as high as possible with the fingertips of both hands, is recommended. Start with ten jumps in succession, maintaining the same height, and then see just how many you can manage without stopping or losing height. This will develop muscular endurance in the legs. Ankle weights are worn to put an overload on the leg muscles, which should ensure extra development of strength and power too.

Strong hands and fingers are needed for good ball control. The skills of passing, dribbling and shooting often require fingertip ball control. For fingertip strength and dexterity try squeezing a rubber ball or use Play Dough (obtainable from toy shops), which is recommended by physiotherapists for those who have had hand injuries; it is both remarkably effective and a convenient exercise which you can do at odd times of the day.

English Basketball Association coaches believe that weight training should be an important component in a player's conditioning programme. They advise their players to evaluate their strengths and weaknesses, so that improvements can be made. Time is spent on exercising and practising techniques perfectly and on the practice of tactical moves. Those techniques and skills will be of little use if players lack the strength and endurance to sustain a high level of skill throughout the game and here it must be emphasised that a programme of progressive resistance exercises will be needed to develop the appropriate muscles. Remember that even if you do not have a star player who is seven feet tall, one of lesser stature with greater leg power can still achieve greater heights in jumping.

A thorough conditioning programme in the off-season and early pre-season should ensure that there are fewer incapacitating injuries such as sore shins and weak ankles.

Suggested weight training routine for basketball players:

1	Warm-up and stretching routine
2	Bent-over rowing (dorsal exercise, p.53)
3	Squat jumps (leg exercise, p.47)
4	Arm curls (arm and shoulder exercise, p.38)
5	Calf raise (leg exercise, p.52)
6	Bench press (chest exercise, p.56)
7	Trunk curls (abdominal exercise, p.45)
8	Military press (arm exercise, p.44)
9	Straight arm pullover (chest exercise, p.57)

Cricket

Three vital physical attributes for cricketers today are: skill, stamina and speed. Standards of play have improved tremendously and with this has come the recognition of the fact that players have to be extremely fit and alert. If you are tired and out of breath because you are not fit, you will not be able to concentrate for more than an hour. Fatigue plays tricks with your mind and takes it away from the match.

Cricket can be a hard game. Bowlers take a lot of strain in the groin muscles and those of the back and shoulders. All these muscles need special care in stretching as well as strengthening. As a bowler you will come to accept that an arduous training programme is part of your year. Some fast bowlers now put themselves through a special stretching routine immediately before going onto the pitch – resting one leg on a table and slowly straightening the leg to its full extent. Specific fitness training for cricket is essential. Sarah Potter, a left-arm fast bowler for England and also a county hockey player, trains with weights between the end of the cricket season and the beginning of the hockey season.

There is no one programme that suits all players: use a commonsense approach and work out the routine that suits you best.

Suggested weight training routine for cricketers:

1	Warm-up and stretching
2	Arm curls (arm exercise, p.38)
3	Half squat (leg exercise, p.48)
4	Trunk curls with legs raised (abdominal exercise, p.46)
5	Leg extension with ankle weights (leg exercise, p.51)
6	Wrist curls (arm exercise, p.40)
7	Bench press (chest exercise, p.56)
8	Triceps extension standing (arm exercise, p.42)
9	Squat jumps (leg exercise, p.47)
10	Squeezing a rubber ball at frequent intervals during the day

Cycle racing

Despite the fact that high-tech has taken over in cycle racing with lightweight molybdenum frames, sophisticated gearing, alloy crank sets and narrow gauge tyres, there are still two elements which remain exactly the same as they were in 1903 when Henri Desranges founded the first six-day cycle race over 1500 miles, the Tour de France. They are the need for strong legs and cardio-vascular fitness.

Cycling is one of the most demanding of all sports. For example, time triallists require a great deal of strength and both kinds of stamina to achieve optimal speed and maintain it for anything up to twenty-four hours. Road racing demands endurance and strength for it challenges the rider with varying racing conditions and terrain. Since some events last for several days, you have to train your body to recover quickly.

Guidelines for the racing cyclist's weight training programme are clearly set out in the authoritative book of the sport written by two former racing cyclists, Frank Westell and Ken Evans.[†] They write: 'One of the best ways of getting stronger is through a strictly controlled weight training programme.' They stress the need for the guidance of an experienced coach who can assess your personal needs and design a programme that will ensure your training is progressive.

When the advice of a coach is not readily available then make sure that you keep a careful watch on your training record so that there is a balance between on-the-bike and off-the-bike training. For example, although your bike work will usually develop leg strength and stamina you will benefit from special leg-power exercises.

The demands of cycle racing are such that very high levels of individual skill, tactical awareness and mental toughness are needed as well as natural ability. The days are long gone when a racing cyclist could say that 'getting the miles in' was all the training anyone needed. Develop your stamina through circuit training (*see also* Chapter 8). As Westell and Evans say: 'Circuit training is tough. If you don't find it tough, then you aren't trying hard enough.'

For those just starting, keep the weights light enough to enable you to develop the correct technique of handling the equipment. Use the three sets technique of ten exercises and then increase the weight that can be handled comfortably at eight repetitions. Weight training is recommended for development of the abdominals, back, arms and shoulders.

There will always be occasions when you want to draw upon your reserves of power; training for power will involve using heavy weights as part of your programme. At this stage the advice of your cycle racing coach is desirable – and you will probably be in a local club.

[†]*Cycle Racing*, Frank Westell and Ken Evans, Springfield Books, 1991

Suggested weight training routine for cyclists:

1	Arm curls (arm exercise, p.38)
2	Bench press (chest exercise, p.56)
3	Half squats (leg exercise, p.48)
4	Straight arm pullovers (chest exercise, p.57)
5	Overhead press (arm exercise, p.44)
6	Trunk raising backwards (dorsal exercise, p.54)
7	Bent over rowing (dorsal exercise, p.53)
8	Inclined curls or cruncher with twist (abdominal exercise, p.47)
9	The lunge (leg exercise, p.49)

Fencing

Fencing is one of the fastest growing sports of today. Newly appointed Development Officers say it is a sport for everyone from five to seventy and even beyond that too. But what they also say, however, is that it is a sport for which you have to be extremely fit, especially for competitions. In particular you have to have powerful leg muscles, a well-developed shoulder girdle, strong wrists and quick reflexes. Anyone who has watched a fiercely contested match will know that players need an abundance of stamina. What is not perhaps realised is that successful players have powerful postural muscles which can react quickly for the maintenance of balance and provision of stability. For example, the lunge, a basic stance in fencing, is dependent on good balance because of the accuracy and speed required in an attack and the necessity for a quick recovery. If the fencer attempts a lunge whilst off balance, the attack will be weak and easily parried – the recovery slow and unsteady.

The conditioning programme for fencers should aim at:

- Strengthening the muscles of arm, shoulder, wrist and legs
- Developing cardio-vascular endurance
- Developing strength and stamina of the postural muscles

Suggested weight training routine for fencing:

1	Warm-up and stretching
2	Overhead press (arm exercise, p.44)
3	Barbell lunges (leg exercises, p.49)
4	Trunk bending sideways with barbell (dorsal exercise, p.54)
5	Calf raise (leg exercise, p.52)
6	Triceps extension (arm exercise, p.42)
7	Squat jumps (leg exercise, p.47)
8	Trunk raising backwards (dorsal exercise, p.54)
9	Wrist curls (arm exercise, p.40)
10	Trunk curls (abdominal exercise, p.45)

Since the game, with its relatively light foils, will not develop all-round body strength and yet requires it for success, weight training is being used increasingly as a means of developing strength and endurance especially during the off-season period.

Golf

Most women who take up golf find that although they may already have strong shoulders and supple hips, they can benefit from a comprehensive weight training routine directed specifically at developing fitness for golf.

Golf is one sport where a smaller person, man or woman, has an ideal opportunity to achieve championship honours if he or she possesses powerful wrists and shoulders. Gary Player, one of the smallest golfers to win the Grand Slam, stayed at the top of his profession for many years, and attributed his success to weight training. Many players have followed his advice and were pleased with the way that it improved their golf handicaps.

It is well known that many professionals use weight training as a means of keeping themselves match fit as well as for preventing injuries and for rehabilitation. One of the prime objectives of a weight training routine is to build up the flexibility and strength of the most frequently used muscles, particularly those of the rotator cuff – the four muscles of the shoulder – so as to reduce the risk of injuries.

Suggested weight training routine for golfers:

1	Warm-up and stretch
2	Lateral raise (arm exercise, p.41)
3	Trunk raising backwards with weight (dorsal exercise, p.54)
4	Trunk curls with twist, legs raised (abdominal exercise, p.46)
5	Wrist curls (arm exercise, p.40) and squeezing a rubber ball
6	Upright rowing (arm exercise, p.40)
7	Trunk bending sideways with barbell (dorsal exercise, p.54)
8	Press behind the neck with barbell (arm exercise, p.43)

Gymnastics

Gymnastics is a sport you would normally take up at an early age, following a programme of intensive coaching and physical conditioning. It requires determination and dedication. The precision needed by gymnasts depends upon a high level of strength and skill. Total muscular endurance is of paramount importance too. In fact gymnasts have to be fitter than participants in almost every other sport. Training, however, has to be finely balanced so that adequate time is spent preparing the gymnast for a wide range of skills and body movements. Strength, stamina and suppleness are of prime importance. You have to know your body's capabilities and its weaknesses, then work on them so you can give a consistent performance in any discipline.

Suggested weight training routine for gymnasts:

```
1   Warm-up and stretch
2   Bench press (chest exercise, p.56)
3   Squat jumps (leg exercise, p.47)
4   Bent arm sideways raise (chest exercise, p.57)
5   Leg extension (leg exercise, p.51)
6   Trunk twisting and lowering backwards (abdominal exercise,
    p.46)
7   Overhead press (arm exercise, p.44)
8   Calf raise (leg exercise, p.52)
9   Straight arm pullover (chest exercise, p.57)
10  Trunk curls with twist (abdominal exercise, p.46)
```

Hockey and lacrosse

Despite the fact that hockey and lacrosse are old-established team games, exciting and a pleasure to watch, they have received little publicity or support from the media. Nevertheless the standard of play has steadily improved during the last decade and performances of British teams have been better than ever before. In both games players have to have the power and endurance to execute skilful movements accurately for the full period of the game, even when fatigued.

As we have already seen with other sports, specific fitness only comes after the body has been conditioned to endure continuous running interspersed with violent bursts of activity, often under pressure, and yet still produce the skills of the game. When stamina is lacking, fatigue soon begins to impair performance. Power, the combination of speed and strength, is essential for sudden changes of direction, for evading an opponent and, of course for shooting hard.

When training for both hockey and lacrosse you must always remember the two kinds of stamina to be developed: cardio-vascular and local muscular. It is the intense physical exertion which causes the heart and lungs to work at a maximum and over long periods fatigue sets in. Local muscular endurance is needed when your muscles must maintain prolonged activity. Sometimes the accumulation of the waste products of fatigue causes the muscles to go into a painful spasm of contraction – cramp. Thus we can have local muscular exhaustion when a player is otherwise fit to carry on playing vigorously. To achieve the strength, speed and power needed by top class hockey and lacrosse players, both circuit training and weight training are recommended.

'To play hockey well today, the pre-season element of training is extremely important,' says Director of coaching for the Hockey Association, John Cadman.[†] He believes that during the playing season, specific training should be planned to maintain, and raise, your overall fitness standard.

For both hockey and lacrosse a strong robust body is a decided asset. It should not be forgotten either that as with many other games, flexibility and agility are important aspects of total fitness.

Suggested weight training routine for hockey and lacrosse:

1	Warm-up and stretching
2	Trunk curls (abdominal exercise, p.45)
3	Lateral raise (arm exercise, p.41)
4	Wrist curls (arm exercise, p.40)
5	The lunge (leg exercise, p.49)
6	Upright rowing (arm exercise, p.40)
7	Squat jump (leg exercise, p.47)
8	Triceps extension (arm exercise, p.42)

Judo

So great is the following for judo and so high are the standards set that it was accepted as a demonstration sport in the Olympics of 1988 and it has full status on the 1992 Olympic calendar.

What is particularly interesting to note is that right from the first interest shown by women in judo, women have practised with men in club sessions. The reasoning behind this is that judo was developed from the fundamental credo that a small man can overturn a much bigger one by skilful application of judo techniques. If this is true then what arguments could be raised against a women competing on the same terms?

This argument is only true, of course, if there should be a major-discrepancy in the level of skills; nevertheless it is interesting to speculate that women will not be disadvantaged when matched against men provided they have a high level of skill and have followed a rigorous course of training to develop their stamina and muscular power.

Weight training is an important part of conditioning programmes for judo enthusiasts. The manager and coach of British women's judo teams, 6th Dan Roy Inman, found that: 'there was a substantial and almost immediate benefit in groundwork practice among the women who had worked with weights . . . the long term effect of increased strength factors meant that, at last, some of the women could realistically begin to attempt important contest throws'.[‡]

[†]*Hockey*, John Cadman, Crowood Press, 1985
[‡]*Judo for Women*, Roy Inman with Nicholas Soames, Crowood Press, 1987

For the development of any new skill a certain level of fitness is needed. As Roy Inman says: 'If a player finds that she cannot do sufficient skill work because she has to keep having a rest, she needs to do some specific work on improving her cardio-vascular state and muscular endurance.' Fitness obtained through practising judo is not enough. Supplementary training is necessary. An important part of this will be weight training.

As with all weight training schedules, do keep a record of your training programme and balance your weight training with working on your judo skills.

Suggested weight training routine for judo players:

1	A thorough warm-up and stretching
2	Half squat (leg exercise, p.48)
3	Bench press (chest exercise, p.56)
4	Arm curls (arm exercise, p.38)
5	Bent over rowing (dorsal exercise, p.53)
6	Press behind the neck (arm exercise, p.43)
7	Double bent arm pullover (chest exercise, p.58)
8	Squat jumps (leg exercise, p.47)

Netball

If you enjoy netball and want to improve your game, the message from the advanced netball coach and English international, Betty Galsworthy is that anyone can learn the skills of netball from books and coaches but she then adds: However, to be able to perform them efficiently through-out the whole game, a player must have a high fitness level. She must be able to run, jump, throw, change direction and generally keep up an excellent level of performance under the continual pressure of opponents who are equally as talented. This requires cardio-vascular and muscular endurance, speed, strength, suppleness and mobility: all highly trainable components of fitness.[†]

Specific training is a question of analysing the game, the movements involved and the type of fitness required by players. Play requires intense movements which are short and sharp, followed by periods of short rest. Research has in fact shown that those bursts of activity are usually no more than ten seconds in length, and the majority of them less than half that time. Consequently the training programme for the England team was based upon short bursts of high intensity activity followed by short rests, with the aim of improving cardio-vascular efficiency. Alongside such training were exercises to improve strength and suppleness.

[†]*Netball, the Skills of the Game*, Betty Galsworthy, Crowood Press, 1979

Weight training and circuit training are used to develop strength and power to enable a player to jump higher, throw further and to move with more impact in short bursts. Increasing power and strength will contribute greatly to increases in speed – needed to outrun an opponent or intercept a pass. Exceptional suppleness will help your ability to twist and turn your body, stretch and land off balance and recover quickly. This is a component of fitness which cannot be satisfactorily developed through play alone.

To sum up, whatever you choose to do in your training programme do remember to warm-up, loosen up and stretch muscles and joints through a full range of movement. Use circuit training and weight training to develop specific fitness and stamina; as the playing season approaches make sure that skill work and tactics are given a high profile in the complete programme. Remember too, that your training should be organised to fit into a three-phase programme according to the season. However, it is important that even during the playing season training for strength and power should be continued, for when all the components of your fitness are maintained to a high standard, you will play more efficiently.

Suggested weight training routine for netball players:

1	Warm-up and stretching
2	Squat jumps (leg exercise, p.47)
3	Trunk bending sideways (dorsal exercise, p.54)
4	Trunk curls with twist (abdominal exercise, p.46)
5	The lunge (leg exercise, p.49)
6	Triceps extension (arm exercise, p.42)
7	Bent over rowing (dorsal exercise, p.53)
8	Bench press (chest exercise, p.56)

Rowing and canoeing

Training for competition rowing and canoeing is exceptionally arduous, and the conditioning phases cover the whole of the year. Much time must inevitably be spent on the water, mastering technique. In addition you will have to decide how the remaining time should be allocated between developing strength, stamina and speed.

Great strength is needed for drawing the broad blade of the paddle or oar cleanly through the water with rhythm. In the post-season period heavy weights can be used with few repetitions to develop strength, but as the competitive season approaches lighter weights are better in a stamina training circuit. Cardio-vascular stamina can also be developed by other activities to provide variety. Some coaches take trainees on a run or arrange a strenuous game of basketball immediately after their water training as a means of experiencing the feeling of pushing their physical capabilities to an even greater extent. Weight training can look after the need for strength and power.

Suggested weight training exercises for rowers and canoeists:

1	Warm-up and stretching
2	Bench press (chest exercise, p.56)
3	Triceps extension (arm exercise, p.42)
4	Trunk curls with twist, legs raised (abdominal exercise, p.46)
5	Arm curls (arm exercise, p.38)
6	Trunk raising backwards (dorsal exercise, p.54)
7	Half squat (leg exercise, p.48)
8	Bent over rowing (dorsal exercise, p.53)
9	Wrist curls (arm exercise, p.40)
10	Press behind neck (arm exercise, p.43)

Skiing

Far too many people tackle what is perhaps the most exciting and exhilarating of all sports – skiing – with inadequate physical preparation. Consequently they arrive at their destination raring to go but highly vulnerable to accidents. A seven-year survey of accident victims has shown that 75 per cent of them were people who had done no kind of physical preparation, 20 per cent had exercised only sporadically and only 5 per cent of all accident cases were people who had actively prepared for their skiing. The conclusion is obvious: a period of physical preparation is an effective way of preventing accidents. Doctors frequently say anyone going skiing without preparing for it in any way first is a danger not only to herself but also to other people. In their book, *The Fitness Jungle*, Connolly and Einzig say: 'Skiing is a potentially dangerous sport. Injuries are largely caused by the skier's lack of conditioning.'[†]

If you have not participated much in sport at other times of the year and yet are contemplating a fortnight's skiing holiday, the beginner's weight training programme outlined in Chapter 3 is recommended. Coaches say that circuit training has proved itself to be an ideal way of preparing for a skiing holiday. Instructors offer the following guidelines to beginners for their physical conditioning:

- Warm-up and stretch muscles and joints in their full range before starting strenuous exercise.
- Two or three times a week take vigorous exercise which raises your heart rate to something like 170 times a minute minus your age.
- Pay particular attention to your knee joints.

[†]*The Fitness Jungle*, Connolly and Einzig, Century Hutchinson, 1986

- Exercise sensibly. A programme which is too ambitious can cause strains. Lead up to your skiing fitness gradually.

The point to remember for both beginners and experienced skiers is that if you are in poor physical condition you will never master a perfect technique. Conversely, once you have a good repertoire of skiing skills you can make effective use of them because you have taken the trouble not only to be generally fit but to be specifically skiing-fit.

For the fit and proficient skier specific weight training exercises along with a circuit training schedule can both reassure and motivate. The following exercises are recommended in addition to a general conditioning programme. Naturally, you can tailor your programme to suit yourself.

Suggested weight training routine for skiers:

1 Half squats with a light weight, done at a fairly fast rate, but not so fast that the style of the exercise is lost (leg exercise, p.48)
2 Trunk bending sideways with barbell (dorsal exercise, p.54)
3 Trunk curls with twist (abdominal exercise, p.46)
4 Lateral raise, alternating sideways and forwards (arm exercise, p.41)
5 Bent over rowing, remember to keep the back straight (dorsal exercise, p.53)
6 Squat jumps (increase the number of jumps as fitness improves whilst not sacrificing height) (leg exercise, p.47)

Squash

Squash is a gladiatorial game. 'You have to be fit in squash simply in order to survive, let alone win,' wrote six times world champion Jonah Barrington[†].

Heed the warnings given about being fit enough to play. In a closed squash court with a high temperature the rallies can be very fast and furious, packed with demanding movements and you will soon raise your pulse rate. It is not a game where you can easily coast along at your own pace, even when playing with someone of your own age group and ability. Squash playing alone will not develop your fitness – indeed you need a high level of fitness before you take up the sport.

Training for the game is very much an individual matter; there is no one system that would suit everybody. But there is one aspect of training that nearly all squash players would agree upon: the need to train under pressure. The speed, endurance and intensity of effort involved in squash at the highest level has to be developed through hard work under pressure over a long period. As Barrington himself puts it:

[†]*Murder in the Squash Court*, Jonah Barrington, Stanley Paul, 1982

'The trainee squash player has not simply to work hard; he or she must be put through the wringer.'

You will need need weight training for the upper body, thighs and calves. The schedule given below would meet the requirements of squash coaches like Nasrullah Khan, who believes that strength must be developed in every part of the body. This can be done by following the suggested schedule, and the general endurance, mental toughness and conditioning for work under pressure can be achieved by circuit training against the clock.

The weight training routine below is a vigorous one. Do not attempt to complete all the exercises if signs of physical distress become evident. Progress under pressure, but sensibly and safely too.

Suggested weight training routine for squash players:

1	Warm-up and stretching
2	Wrist curls (arm exercise, p.40)
3	Trunk curls (abdominal exercise, p.45)
4	Trunk raising backwards (dorsal exercise, p.54)
5	Arm curls (arm exercise, p.38)
6	Half squat (leg exercise, p.48)
7	Press behind the neck (arm exercise, p.43)
8	Trunk bending sideways with barbell (dorsal exercise, p.54)
9	The lunge (leg exercise, p.49)
10	Bench press (chest exercise, p.56)

Swimming

The faster an object moves through water, the greater is the resistance. Resistance is powerful opposition because it obeys an inverse square law that is to say, if the swimmer doubles her swimming speed she will have quadrupled the resistance. The need for strength to propel the body through that increasing resistance needs no emphasis. The two ways to address it are to cultivate strength and an aerodynamic physique to overcome the resistance.

Weight training for swimmers should not only cater for the development of strength and endurance but also suppleness. Most coaches favour weight training to give extra power needed to overcome water resistance, but some coaches are doubtful of the benefits because they feel the use of weights might impair mobility by shortening the muscles, thus restricting mobility of the joints. This is something the swimmer would have to decide for herself. One thing is certain: swimming alone will not bring the required degree of muscle strength needed for maximum performance.

A weight training routine for all swimmers is suggested below; light-weights can be used for increasing suppleness with exercises.

> 1 Double arm circling, holding a ten-pound disc in each hand. Circle forwards and then backwards, keeping the arms as close to the ears as possible
> 2 Trunk bending sideways with light barbell (dorsal exercise, p.54)
> 3 Triceps extension (arm exercise, p.42)
> 4 The lunge, lunging in a variety of ways forwards, sideways, rear leg straight or bent (leg exercises, p.49)
> 5 Upright rowing (arm exercise, p.40)
> 6 Squat jumps using a very light weight and concentrating on getting as high as possible and extending the ankles (leg exercise, p.47)

For developing strength and power the swimmer should use heavy weights with few repetitions:

> 1 Straight arm pullovers (chest exercise, p.57)
> 2 Trunk curls (abdominal exercise, p.45)
> 3 Bench press (chest exercise, p.56)
> 4 Triceps extension, seated (arm exercise, p.42)
> 5 Half squat (leg exercise, p.48)
> 6 Press behind the neck (arm exercise, p.43)
> 7 Trunk raising backwards (dorsal exercise, p.54)
>
> When progress has been made with dorsal strength then the exercise can be done with arms raising backwards whilst holding light weights.

Tennis

Tennis is both a social and professional sport, and in both spheres competition can be very fierce. Careful conditioning routines are needed by those who wish to win competitions, because just playing tennis does not cultivate flexibility for scooping low shots off the surface, rotating to retrieve impossible shots nor for changing direction suddenly. Neither will it develop the strength and stamina needed for top-class matches which might last for several hours, thereby requiring you to be in excellent physical condition.

Naturally, technical ability is of the highest importance and time must be spent in developing this, but for those who have a driving urge to succeed, a strict and specific conditioning schedule is necessary. Remember too that being at your peak of physical fitness for the sport brings the bonus of confidence; this self-confidence has been evident time and time again in champions. They feel they have the physical capacity to use their skills to optimal advantage and they go on to win.

The key to successful tennis fitness training is moderation, with training aimed at developing automatic motor response, stamina and speed. Strenuous endurance and heavy weight training activities should be avoided in the days immediately preceding serious competitions.

Suggested weight training routine for tennis players:

```
1   Warm-up and stretch
2   Wrist curls (arm exercise, p.40)
3   Bench press (chest exercise, p.56)
4   Trunk raising backwards (dorsal exercise, p.54)
5   Squat jumps (leg exercise, p.47)
6   Straight arm pullovers (chest exercise, p.57)
7   Trunk curls with and without twist (abdominal exercise, p.46)
8   Arm curls (arm exercise, p.38)
9   Triceps extension (arm exercise, p.42)
```

Volleyball

In the 1970s the 'Sport for All' campaign launched by the Sports Council of Great Britain gave a boost to many of the lesser-known team games. Televising of these games at international level gave further impetus to their growth. One of these fast-growing sports was volleyball. Even on the beach – where many of us are first introduced to the game – it is highly competitive, requiring a great deal of skill and endurance. When analysing the physical requirements to play volleyball well the first factor that comes to mind is that you must be able to occupy every position and therefore need the physical attributes and skills to cover each position well. Weight training is an obvious way of helping players to acquire a high degree of fitness, particularly in agility and power.

Suggested weight training routine for volleyball players:

```
1    Warm-up and stretch
2    Squat jumps with weight (leg exercise, p.47)
3    Press behind the neck (arm exercise, p.43)
4    Calf raise (leg exercise, p.52)
5    Trunk bending sideways with barbell (dorsal exercise, p.54)
6    Trunk curls, legs raised (abdominal exercise, p.45)
7    Wrist curls with barbell or dumb-bell (arm exercise, p.40)
8    Triceps extension (arm exercise, p.42)
9    Double bent arm pullover (chest exercise, p.58)
10   Bent over rowing (dorsal exercise, p.53)
```

CHAPTER NINE
Training for athletics – track and field

In athletics there has been a scientific revolution and we are now in the era of the super-athlete. And the more we find out about human performance, the more emphasis there is on a scientific and specific approach to training. This applies not only to the physical conditioning of athletes but also to the psychological approach. Competitors have to adjust to the ups and downs of a long and arduous season, often covering different climates and conditions on different continents.

Naturally, the task of getting fit is much harder in the early stages than when the athlete reaches the stage of honing the competitive edge of her performance. One of the early lessons to be learned is that there is no real period of rest – or if there is, it will be short indeed – once the competition season has ended. In the weeks following the last competition you will learn to participate in phases of 'active recuperation' rather than complete rest, when for a short time you can play other vigorous but non-body contact games where injuries are less likely. In this way you can come back to your pre-season training with a reasonably high baseline of fitness and thus progress more rapidly towards specific fitness for the event.

It is during this post-season period too that many athletes maintain and monitor their general fitness through weight training. Top athletes have to maintain a high standard over a much longer period than some sportspeople, so the off-season training is particularly important. As one Olympic gold medallist and sports journalist, Chris Brasher, recently wrote in the *Observer*: 'It is the winter training that stores great races into the system.'

Planning your training time

How much training time does it take to make it to the top? The short answer is that it varies considerably with each sport. David Hemery's study of the highest achievers in over twenty sports *Sporting Excellence*, Willow Books, Collins, 1986, revealed that long-distance runners can manage an hour's training at either end of the day, covering a total of twenty miles and that is as much as the body could stand for it to recover sufficiently to do the same distance the following day. Yet ice dance champions Jayne Torvill and Christopher Dean told how they spent six hours on the ice every day to reach their gold medals and a standard of excellence rarely seen. And world pursuit cycling champion, Steel Bishop, also trained for six hours a day, seven days a week.

Such facts prompt the questions: 'What was the intensity of that training?' and 'Were they each giving 100 per cent effort all the time?' Champions in various events and sports gave different answers to those questions. Steel Bishop said he spent the first two hours doing steady distance, rolling along at a training pace of twenty miles an hour. This was followed by two further sessions of intensive effort, each of two hours' duration but with a break for lunch in between. World decathlon champion Daley Thompson always gave 100 per cent in training, and so too did squash champion Jonah Barrington, a keen weight trainer, who based his training on becoming the fittest player in the game. On the other hand, Sebastian Coe, the only athlete to have retained the Olympic 1500m title, rarely gave 100 per cent effort on a training run but always gave it in his conditioning training. Similar responses came from other athletes.

What conclusions can we draw from such varied responses? Some athletes apparently give 100 per cent effort all the time whilst others give it only to certain aspects of their training. The fact is that all the athletes, working to an individual plan, were giving as much as they felt they could demand of themselves.

Heather McKay, the world squash champion, who during her twenty years at the top lost only two games, summed up pointing out that to succeed, anyone would have to go out and make the commitment, whether it was in sport, work, school or marriage. If you only give 40 per cent then you cannot expect 100 per cent in return. The option is yours. 'In many cases, it was the blood, sweat and tears given by those top athletes which made them individual record breakers: they chose to make such efforts,' writes David Hemery in *Sporting Excellence*, and he goes on to make the point that you have to enjoy what you do and be highly motivated.

Winning can thrust, almost overnight, an impecunious 'also-ran' into a millionaire lifestyle, and that in turn can create an insatiable appetite for success. In some, the dedication to training can manifest itself in an inflexibility of will and even a total ruthlessness to carve a path relentlessly to the top: once at the top, it can be tough, mentally and physically.

In athletics, when asking what form of training is needed to get to the top and stay there you will find that opinions differ with field events and with track events. Let us consider them separately.

Field events

Weight training is embodied in the conditioning programmes of nearly all the top women in field event athletics in the world. They know it is the quickest way of developing strength and that for events which involve some heavy resistance to be overcome, strength is the dominating factor influencing performance. Quite dramatic improvements in throwing distances can be achieved after only a few months of weight training, combined with the proper coaching of skills.

Power development for throwing events

Each of the four main throwing events requires power, generated in different ways, but the performance depends principally on the transfer of momentum from the body via the hand to the implement being thrown. For example, in throwing the javelin, momentum is gained initially from the running steps up to the point when the arm is swung back to put the throwing muscles on maximum stretch before the final impelling thrust. Several things then happen at once: prime throwing muscles contract, the body rotates, and the rear leg extends powerfully so that as the javelin leaves the hand, the whole body – arm, trunk and legs, extends in one collected effort. The powerful thrust of the javelin is the cumulative result of a coordinated effort by all the major muscle groups of the body. Hence the need for all-round strength development as well as specific strengthening of the prime throwing muscles.

It requires precise neuro-muscular efficiency to coordinate the actions as they spread across the body, from the legs to the hips, trunk, arm, wrist and fingers. The successful javelin thrower is the one who can make the best use of all these forces. It requires the help of a good coach to make sure that adequate strength is developed, that coordination is superb, and that the style adopted is the most efficient for the individual concerned.

Momentum for discus and hammer throwing cannot rely initially upon a run-up, and the impetus for throwing the discus and hammer must therefore come from the rapidity of the spin – the rotational power of the trunk and leg muscles and the final whipping round of the body for the delivery. Once again, it is the power of the whole body that is unleashed in one explosive effort.

Spin techniques are not possible with the shot, and the power required to thrust the heavy weight forward has to be generated within the confined space of the putting circle. Consequently, great strength of the prime muscles involved has to be developed to overcome inertia and propel the heavy shot; it comes from the rotation of the hips and shoulders, flexion of the shoulder and extension of the arm combined with the extension of the hip and knee. The final impetus is given by the wrist and fingers. The non-throwing arm is also utilised across the body to help with rotation and maintain body balance. The shot putter needs tremendous power in the arms and shoulders as well as in the body and leg muscles.

An important characteristic of good throwers and putters is strength; as in most sports, strength alone is not enough. Speed and agility are very important too. The conditioning programme for athletes wishing to improve their performance in the throwing events should also cater for the development of flexibility, balance and speed. Participation in games such as badminton and squash can help, as well as a regular routine of mobilising and stretching exercises.

A comprehensive conditioning programme for athletes training for field events should have the following aims:
- development of all-round strength and stamina
- co-ordination and development of all muscle groups
- development of agility and flexibility
- practice in skills and technique

Basic weight training schedules for throwing events

There is no single programme that will suffice for all field events; training for both track and field is an individual matter. But the basic schedule suggested is designed to develop all-round strength.

1 Warm-up and stretch
2 Overhead press (arm exercise, p.44)
3 Trunk raising backwards with weights behind neck (dorsal exercise, p.54)
4 Squat jumps (leg exercise, p.47)
5 Bench press (chest exercise, p.56)
6 Trunk bending sideways with barbell (dorsal exercise, p.54)
7 Calf raise (leg exercise, p.52)
8 Upright rowing (arm exercise, p.40)

These exercises should be done with weights which permit no more than about ten repetitions in each set. Special exercises which international athletes have used and found beneficial are shown for the specific events below.

Putting the shot

Certainly no other field event carries with it such an obvious need for strength as does the shot put. Even though the action is primarily a full body movement, as we have seen, the critical need for power is essentially in the arm and shoulder muscles. Many coaches, however, might justifiably argue that leg strength is equally important to ensure that the movement of the shot from its start across the ring until its final release, is one of constant acceleration. Therefore, depending upon your physique, a proportional amount of time should be spent on developing leg muscles as well.

The weight training programme below should lead progressively to exercises of sufficiently high intensity to develop the pushing muscles of the arm and shoulder.

Suggested weight training routine for shot putters:

1	Warm-up and stretching routine
2	Press behind the neck (arm exercise, p.43)
3	Squat jumps (leg exercise, p.47)
4	Arm curls with dumb-bells (arm exercise, p.38)
5	Trunk twisting and lowering backwards (abdominal exercise, p.46)
6	Wrist curls (arm exercise, p.40)
7	Overhead press (arm exercise, p.44)
8	Trunk curls with twist (abdominal exercise, p.46)
9	Double bent arm pullover (chest exercise, p.58)
10	Step-ups (leg exercise, p.50)
11	Triceps extension (arm exercise, p.42)
12	Bent over rowing (dorsal exercise, p.53)

Throwing the javelin

Superior strength in the arm and shoulder muscles is mandatory for throwing the javelin, but it will be relatively ineffective if your skills of throwing and fundamental techniques are not properly co-ordinated.

Suggested weight training routine for throwing:

1	Warm-up and stretching routine
2	Overhead press (arm exercise, p.44)
3	Lateral raise (arm exercise, p.41)
4	Bent arm sideways raise (chest exercise, p.57)
5	Half squats (leg exercise, p.48)
6	Bent over rowing (dorsal exercise, p.53)
7	Trunk twisting and lowering backwards (abdominal exercise, p.46).
8	Straight arm pullover (chest exercise, p.57)
9	Trunk bending sideways with barbell (dorsal exercise, p.54).
10	Wrist curls (arm exercise, p.40)
11	Squat jumps (leg exercise, p.47)

Adequate time must be devoted to this but coaches also point out that because of the peculiar stress on the elbow involved in throwing the javelin, caution is recommended in deciding how many throws at maximum effort can safely be carried out each day so that arm injuries can be prevented. Unusual care in the warming-up session and protection of the throwing arm between trials is urged, especially on cold days.

During your weight training sessions, remember to balance exercises between those muscles used directly in the throw and those that maintain flexibility.

High pulls
Crouch with hands in overgrasp position on the bar in front of you, your feet, tucked under it. Lift and push hard with your legs and drive your body upwards, so that you finish with the bar held high under the chin; rise onto your toes. Slowly lower the barbell to the ground and repeat. This exercise is very good for developing power in the arms and legs, and improves coordination.

Throwing the hammer

The hammer cannot be thrown far without bringing the whole body into the action, in order to overcome the inertia of the heavy object. The complete action involves the legs, hips, trunk, shoulders, arm, forearm and hand. The successful hammer thrower has to ensure that all muscles of the body are strengthened by progressive resistance exercises, as well as making a special effort with the rear fibres of the deltoid and the rhomboids and other dorsal muscles used in the final explosive effort.

As a general rule coaches seem to favour weight training three times a week and no more than once on those days; the number of repetitions and weight lifted is more of a decision for the individual. You can reduce your sessions to once or twice a week during the competitive season according to the way you respond to training and your level of performance.

Throwing the discus

The attainment of maximum distance in throwing the discus requires a sequence of movements; the final effort is a summation of all potential forces extending from the toes to the fingers. The conditioning programme, in the post- and pre-season, must aim at developing the large muscle groups of the legs and trunk, as well as those of the shoulder, arm, wrist and fingers.

Follow the general programme outlined earlier together, with a modified version of the bent arm raise from lying: Modified bent arm raise from lying (chest exercise, p.57)

This develops strength in the pectorals and in the anterior fibres of the deltoid. The best effects are achieved when the exercise is done from a high bench or the top of a vaulting box so that the arms and hands holding the dumb-bells are high enough to fall back as far as possible without touching the ground. The pectoral and deltoid muscles are then worked from a stretched position. If the elbows are bent slightly then a heavier weight can be handled safely. Bring the weights together above the chest as with the bent arm raise exercise.

From the same raised box the double bent arm pullover exercise can also be done (chest exercise, p.58)

Training for jumping events

Both the sprinter and the long jumper aim to project their bodies forward with maximum velocity. Many excellent sprinters have found that despite possessing a powerful spring they still fail to gain the distance in the long jump that they would expect to from having good physical condition. This is probably due to a lack of neuro-muscular coordination, which can be corrected by a good coach – as can a lack of muscular power. The successful long jumper must aim to acquire the speed of the sprinter as part of a good technique.

The technique of a sucessful high jumper propels the body straight upwards and over the bar. Although the objectives are different in the two types of jump, the power for the jumps is generated by the same muscle groups. Specific training should aim at developing strength in the extensors of the ankle, knee and hip, and the flexors of the thigh.

Suggested weight training routine for jumping events:

1	Warm-up and stretching and flexibility routine
2	Half squat (leg exercise, p.48)
3	Trunk curls with twist (abdominal exercise, p.46)
4	Trunk raising backwards (dorsal exercise, p.54)
5	Straight arm pullover (chest exercise, p.57)
6	Barbell lunge (leg exercise, p.49)
7	Calf raise with barbell (leg exercise, p.52)
8	Trunk bending sideways with barbell (dorsal exercise, p.54)
9	Lateral raise forwards and also sideways (arm exercises, p.41)
10	Bent over rowing (dorsal exercise, p.53)
11	Leg extension (leg exercise, p.51)
12	Leg curls (leg exercise, p.51)

Your muscles, rarely work independently: prime movers work ineffi-ciently if those muscles which fix and stabilise joints are not capable of correspondingly strong actions. Therefore it would be wrong for jumpers to concentrate entirely upon developing just the prime movers listed above. The chest and abdominal muscles play an important part in the upward thrust, as do the muscles of the arms. Muscles controlling posture, as we have seen earlier, are important too; jumpers have to maintain balance during flight to achieve maximum distance and an efficient landing.

Track events

Once the track season has begun some coaches recommend that weight training is taken out of the training programme for the whole of the competitive season. National athletics coaches John le Masurier and Dennis Watts in their book *Athletics – Track Events*, A and C Black, 1980, say: 'The best training for running is running – there is no doubt about that, but an hour or so of weight training each week can prove extremely useful'. Being more specific, they go on: 'For the sprinter and hurdler, weight training provides extra strength and 'explosiveness' in the muscles used for starting and running at top speed. For the middle and long distance runner it can add strength to the chest, arms and abdomen to complement strength and endurance built up in the legs.'

Draw up a comprehensive plan, assisted by your coach, so that the appropriate components of specific fitness receive special attention whilst that technique needed to utilise additional strength and stamina is developed too. The number of weight training exercises included in the conditioning programme and the frequency of their repetition then becomes a matter for the individual athlete.

As mentioned, the argument as to whether running endurance is best achieved simply through running on the track, road, or across country, goes on. Long-distance runners will certainly develop endurance and cross-country events are often used by track men as a winter conditioning programme. But endurance does not affect speed, and essentially the runner who wins the race is the one who can run the distance in the fastest possible time. Speed is the yardstick of success.

Developing speed

To have speed there must be power. The basis of power is strength. The rough explanation goes like this: forward motion of running – as shown on a slow-motion film – comprises a series of propulsive thrusts by the rear leg as it forcibly extends against the ground. The legs are brought alternately under the body to give a moment or two of support in between each forward thrust. Following this line of argument, it can be seen that the rear leg is projecting the body weight – say 150 pounds – forwards and upwards in the same way as the shot putter's arm projects the shot. The difference is that the legs propel your body weight in quick succession over a given period of time – the length of the race. As the speed of the runner increases, her body weight is projected forwards and upwards clear of the ground for a greater distance and longer period of time until eventually, when the top speed is reached, the period of support in between each successive drive from the rear leg is very brief.

If we were to examine further the slow-motion film of running it would show the athlete's legs exerting a far greater force against the ground during the first twenty to forty metres. When the body is inclined forwards, the stride is shorter and more staccato than when the maximum speed has been reached and a more erect running angle of the body adopted. This analysis could also be supported by looking at the footprints left in the track by runners' feet; they are more noticeable and closer together than during the accelerating period. Once the runner has gained maximum speed the marks on the track are further apart and efforts are directed towards moving the limbs rapidly and maintaining a longer stride. You need muscle strength to do this.

Strength is needed for two purposes: first, to provide the initial power to propel the body weight through the air from the starting blocks and second to move your legs rapidly between each successive thrust. This calls for a quick swing forward, check of momentum and rapid change of direction to swing back again.

Training for running strength and power

The main power for sprinting comes from the muscles of the thighs and buttocks, but an important ancillary thrust comes from the calf muscles which extend down to the ankles, and it is this final vigorous push from the ankles that increases the length of the stride which in itself will increase speed.

Some coaches advise weight training routines which include such exercises as arm curls and the overhead press; the arms, despite having no external resistance to overcome in moving the body forward, do have to swing against the alternating rotary movements of the body, so that shoulders do not swing in the same direction as the hips and therefore the arm and shoulder muscles are in fact working against the other strong muscle groups of the body. Strong back, shoulder and neck muscles ensure that the primary muscles used in running have a firm base from which to work.

We have only to look closely at the action of a tired runner to see the changes that take place when fatigue and strain begin to take their toll. The weary runner will allow her shoulders and neck to wobble; her head will sink backwards. The head, a weighty object, has a considerable effect upon the whole balance of the body. When it sags backwards onto the shoulders the angle of the body lean is affected and this in itself has an adverse effect upon running style and mechanical efficiency. The length of the stride is cut, which causes the driving action of the legs to be reduced to prevent the athlete from falling off balance. Clearly, there has got to be strength for stability, as well as for propulsion.

Once your optimum strength has been reached then your weight training programme can be dropped or used just for maintaining that level of strength already acquired, and more time can be spent in running – on style, race tactics and the development of endurance.

Specific training requirements for different running events

A very high degree of proficiency in running needs so many refinements that most of the top athletes in track events have to train for many years to acquire the fundamentals of good running performance, and the techniques required may vary from one event to another. For marathon running the most relaxed of styles is needed – there is very little thrusting action to be seen in the arms and legs. Middle- and long-distance runners need physical as well as mental stamina plus a reserve of strength and power to accelerate into a final spurt if necessary, whereas in sprinting there is aggression and hard effort. Sprinters have to overcome inertia in the shortest possible time and to accelerate rapidly they need strong responsive muscles. The marathon runner need waste no effort on rapid acceleration.

Because of differences in style between long distance runners and sprinters, training methods must differ too. Weight training can help considerably to meet these needs. Stamina can be developed by circuit training and by other running activities: leg strength can be improved by using heavy weights with few repetitions, and mental stamina will improve during the training period as a direct result of confidence gained through battling with increasing poundages and repetitions. Ultimately this mental stamina will be self-renewing, as a result of persevering with a rigorous training routine and of noting how the body can overcome signals of distress, and also from graded experience in highly competitive and evenly matched races and by winning. The major part of your weight training routines can be done during the winter months so that once the competitive season begins there should be little need for it.

Conditioning programmes for sprinters should be designed to develop the strength and power for the initial explosive thrust that coincides with the explosion of the cartridge in the starting pistol; the response must be instantaneous. The coordination of mind and muscle necessary for immediate response can only be acquired by an athlete who is superbly fit. Physiologists claim that progressive weight training enables the nervous system to discharge motor impulses into the muscles at a greater frequency. A greater proportion of the muscle fibres can be stimulated too.

Training schedules for sprinters should be directed first of all to the development of optimum strength and then towards the coordination of mind and muscle for the start and good running style during the race. Good style will also call for supple hips.

Coaches find with most young sprinters there is a need to improve the range of movement generally in order to achieve a free-flowing action. Therefore flexibility routines should not be neglected. Top-class sprinters run lifting the thigh high and with full extension of the hip, knee and ankle joints. You need suppleness and good flexiblity to do this: the more powerful the muscles which extend the legs, the more effective will be the stride.

Suggested weight training routine for sprinters:

> 1 Warm-up and stretching routines
> 2 Half squats (leg exercise, p.48)
> 3 Trunk raising backwards (dorsal exercise, p.54)
> 4 Trunk curls with twist, legs raised (abdominal exercise, p.46)
> 5 Straight arm pullovers (chest exercise, p.57)
> 6 Calf raise (leg exercise, p.52)
> 7 Step-ups (leg exercise, p.50) Although this exercise is usually associated with a routine for developing general endurance it is a first class exercise for sprinters because it develops the extensors of the leg and the hip flexors, responsible for the high knee lift. Use a bench or a chair at least 50cm high.

If you are a beginner you are advised to proceed with caution in your conditioning programme and also with track activities, especially in the early part of the season. You should not, for example, participate in starts with the pistol and striding at full effort until you are physically in shape for such spasmodic activity. A thorough warm-up and stretching routine should help to minimise the risk of injuries.

Middle-distance runners

In addition to progressive resistance exercises using weights, some runners incorporate other kinds of exercise resistance in their winter training, such as 'sandhill running' – a succession of uphill sprints, or cross country running over soft ground, running through snow and even running with a weighted belt or 'heavy hands'.

For their conditioning programme many athletes adopt, initially, a heavy and light weight training routine. Some sets of the exercises are done with heavy weights and few repetitions, followed by a set with lighter weights and many repetitions. Other coaches favour a heavy routine for the early winter months, followed by a light one as the competitive season approaches. If you are in some doubt consult your coach or local club.

Suggested weight training routine for middle-distance runners:

1	Warm-up and stretching routines
2	Squat jumps (leg exercise, p.47)
3	Bent arm sideways raise (chest exercise, p.57)
4	Calf raise (leg exercise, p.52)
5	The lunge try both types, with rear leg straight and rear leg bent (leg exercises, p.49)
6	Trunk curls with legs raised (abdominal exercise, p.46)
7	Upright rowing (arm exercise, p.40)
8	Bench press (chest exercise, p.56)
9	Leg extension (leg exercise, p.51)
10	Trunk bending sideways with barbell (dorsal exercise, p.54)

The programme yielding the most satisfactory results will be a balanced one in which training for speed, agility, flexibility and endurance receive an adequate allocation of time.

Long-distance runners

The style of long- and middle-distance runners is somewhat different. For long-distance running the angle of the trunk from the vertical position is less than that of a middle-distance runner and they do not incline forward quite as much; the arm action is less vigorous and is swung in a more relaxed manner, the hands are lightly cupped and the legs stride out in a smooth rhythmic movement. The action is aimed at covering the distance quickly yet at the same time conserving energy.

One difference in conditioning programmes for long-distance runners and sprinters, is the care of their feet, not just with regard to footwear and hygiene, but that exercises for the feet should be done, so as to reduce the risk of injuries to the arches.

Final comment

To be successful in any sphere, good time management is essential. With athletics, the first step in developing effective time management is to set clearly defined aims and objectives to be reached on the way to the ultimate aim. Those intermediate objectives or goals have got to be realistic, and to be able to do this properly you have to decide what your priorities are; there is always so much to be done and so little time!

Throughout this book the importance of flexibility as well as strength and endurance has been stressed. Joint flexibility is extremely important for all women competing in track and field events.

CHAPTER TEN

Slimming through weight training

Do you recognise these quotations? 'Do your family responsibilities and your work keep you too occupied to do anything about your figure and fitness? Do you find aerobics, jazz dancing and jogging too strenuous and time-consuming? Then read about a new method . . . .' such are the eye-catching headlines of advertisements for yet another revolutionary piece of equipment promising 'a firmer stomach in weeks', a 'truly amazing way to trim your figure' with, apparently, very little effort at all on your part. Such sales talk plays on your guilty conscience, pointing out your bulges and expanding waistline. Not surprisingly, such 'amazing equipment' is always light enough to be sent to you through the post and is a bargain! But you do not need any gimmicky equipment nor revolutionary diets. The truth is that over a number of years an overweight body will have deposited excess fat in the hip and thigh area where it can be stored without causing too much hardship for its owner. You cannot reverse the process overnight. You need to tip the balance between calorie input and output so that it works favourably for you with minimal expenditure of time and effort. You can do this by:

- increasing your energy expenditure, exercising effectively more than you have been doing
- eating less: take smaller portions or leave food on your plate, and not on your waistline

To this simple piece of advice your answer might well be: 'I'm shattered enough at the end of each day without having to exercise as well. I'd never manage that.' And so you might be tempted to look for an easier way of burning up fat, such as those mentioned earlier, or claims from women who have succeeded by making dramatic changes in their diet regimes, by increasing that mysterious factor, the 'metabolic rate'.

Can you increase your metabolic rate?

Dr Andrew Prentice thinks not. He and his colleagues have been engaged in researching this matter of exercise, diet and weight changes over a number of years and, when speaking on *BBC Radio Four* on 17

May 1991, he had this to say:

> Publications that talk of boosting metabolism are simply trying to add spice to a rather dull message and could confuse the desperate dieter grasping at some simple remedy. I think it is very misleading to sell the idea that there are easy ways of losing weight. Where is the scientific evidence that supports the claims that you can increase metabolic rate by changing your diet? We spend our lives working on these problems of weight loss and cannot find anything that supports that claim. If metabolic rate is increased that energy has got to go somewhere, it's got to appear as heat and if special diets for increasing metabolic rate had any significant effect upon that rate then the people on these diets would be getting red hot. That's the only thing that can happen. That's a physical law.

We do not need any hyped-up, 'revolutionary' mail-order-packaged equipment nor any dramatic new diet in order to resculpture hips and thighs. We can do this most effectively with two or three weight training sessions a week expending energy fuel and by adopting a sensible weight-reducing diet. Of this you can be assured; there are routines which can help everybody to regain their shape. But tackle the job sensibly.

If you are fortunate enough to be slim, then it will pay dividends to stay that way. But as time passes there are many pressures to contend with and it is not surprising that we sometimes forget to service our bodies with the same care that we might lavish upon a car. We all know that it is easier to keep lean and slim than it is to take off excess fat once it has been allowed to build up over the years. But some people continue to eat more than they need so that they can no longer get into clothes they once wore comfortably. And they carry so much extra weight that they can no longer do all those things they formerly took in their stride. Frankly, the reasons why we do these things must be looked at honestly before any exercise and diet programme can succeed in the long term.

Why do people get fat?

'It's my glands!' 'I eat like a bird!' 'I'm just made that way!' 'Diets and exercise have absolutely no effect upon me!' You've no doubt heard people expressing such sentiments. There is no medical support for these theories either. Overeating and lack of exercise are the cause of 90 per cent of all cases of being over-weight. Medical opinion states categorically that only rarely is the condition attributable to inactivity of the ductless glands – thyroid, pituitary or sex glands.

There is another myth about gaining and losing weight too. It is that skinny people have some sort of mechanism which burns off calories more quickly than other people. Of this old canard, Dr Andrew Prentice said: 'We put this theory to the test by taking a sample of skinny people and over-feeding them with massive meals. All that happened was that they gained a huge amount of weight.'

Consider yourself: if you are lean and lithe do not take it for granted. You need to keep active. If you are beginning to gain too much weight think about how you first noticed yourself getting fatter. Have your eating habits changed? When the cause is understood then the cure is easier to undertake. Work out exactly what weight you want to be and how many pounds you need to shed.

What is your ideal weight?

It is sometimes said that the ideal weight for a woman is her weight on her twenty-fifth birthday, but this is not always true, for a variety of reasons. Furthermore, defining accurate ideal weights for age and height is also difficult because body types vary. Some women are bigger-boned than others and therefore have a larger frame to cover with fat and muscle. Consequently on the chart showing ideal weights for size and age, an allowance of 10 per cent either way can be made for different body types. To be absolutely sure – and if you are worried about whether you are carrying too much fat or not – ask your doctor for guidance. Only he can tell you accurately what you ought to weigh by comparing your body type with detailed medical charts for average weights and ages.

You do not need to look fat to be overweight. Excess poundage can creep on insidiously, with the passing years and can become a threat to your health. So you could be overweight without realising it. Shedding this excess can bring a level of well-being and vitality which you have long forgotten, or have never previously enjoyed. Try these tests:

- Is it harder for you to squeeze into clothes you wore last year?
- Pinch the flesh on the back of your upper arm midway between your shoulder and elbow. If it is more than an inch thick you are too fat.

Shaping up with weights

For those who like scientific statistics, physiologists say that approximately 3,500 calories taken surplus to energy requirements would be stored as a pound of fat. So, if 100 calories are not used as energy fuel each day for thirty-five days, then your body will have one extra pound of fat to carry as you go about your daily tasks.

The equation of input and output works cumulatively. If you eat an extra slice of bread (1½ ounces) each day, above your energy requirements, this could add about ten pounds of fat onto your body frame each year. Correspondingly, to lose ten pounds a year, you only need to create an energy deficit of 35,000 calories or 100 calories a day.

Diet and exercise should go hand in hand. Exercise is additionally important in taking off the inches by firming up the musculature beneath the layers of fat. Oddly enough, though all the facts about dieting and exercise have been fairly common knowledge for a number of years, it is only recently that women have realised that minutes spent exercising with weights are far more effective in calorie consumption than most other forms of exercise.

Perhaps one of the attractions of weight training is that you can actually measure your progress physically each week and you can log your exercise in terms of weight lifted and time spent.

It is not absolutely essential to use barbells or dumb-bells to give your body exercise against resistance; you can make use of your body's own weight by doing exercises which cause muscles to lift part or all of the body's weight as, for example, in press ups against a kitchen worktop or on the floor if you feel strong enough. We must not forget either, that your leg muscles, comprising two-thirds of the body's total musculature, are working very hard to carry perhaps 140 pounds or more of body weight as you walk, whilst the muscles of posture are also working to balance the body weight upon alternating points of balance above your feet.

There are immense benefits to be gained from weight training in a slimming campaign. We can compare the energy expenditure in walking with weight training: you would have to walk for a much longer time to consume the same amount of energy as would be used in a few minutes of exercising with weights.

But by carrying your own extra weights held in the hands, or in a rucksack, you can effectively boost your slimming regime.

Calories burned in walking for an hour

Speed of walking (mph)	Body weight (in pounds)					
	100	120	140	160	180	220
2	130	160	185	210	240	290
2½	155	185	220	250	280	345
3	180	215	250	285	325	395
3½	205	248	290	330	375	455
4	235	280	325	375	420	515
4½	310	370	435	495	550	680

Looking at the table showing calories burnt in normal walking, and at various speeds, you can see how extra weight carried throws additional work upon the leg muscles (anyone who has carried a tired child can vouch for this), and then consider how you could easily add 200 calories worth of exercise a day, and more, simply through two twenty-minute sessions of brisk walking to and from work or the shops. Not to mention the saving in travelling expenses!

Will exercise with weights increase my appetite?

Indolent cynics can often be heard to say that exercising is a self-defeating activity for slimmers because muscle work stimulates the appetite and you eat more. This, they say, leads to weight increase through eating more calories than are actually expended in the course of physical activity. This argument has no scientific validity. Unless you are greedy, the opposite is more likely to be true. Experience and medical research suggest that weight training, and other forms of exercise, including walking, can curb the appetite. Taking vigorous exercise does not necessarily mean that you will want to eat a bigger meal afterwards. In fact, what happens is the more physically active you are, the more your appetite is reflexively adjusted, so that you take in no more food than you actually need. Strenuous physical activity can subdue your appetite.

Armed with this information Jean Niditch, who founded Weight Watchers, advised her clients to take a walk whenever they felt a craving for food. The same idea is supported by Laurence Morehouse, Professor of Exercise Physiology at the University of Los Angeles, who writes: 'Physical inactivity leads to increased food intake. Cattle raisers know this and pen their stock. The result of inactivity is a rapid gain of body fat and softening of muscle tissue.'[†] Do not let the cynics put you off with fallacious ideas about increased eating after physical exercise. And remember that weight training is an ideal way of burning calories and if combined with dietary restraint it is surely the most simple way of achieving a debit balance of at least 3500 calories a week and thus losing a pound of fat.

Effective weight control

Losing weight is really only the beginning of an ongoing process of effective weight control. The experience of many women who have attended aerobics classes for a number of weeks is that they lose weight, often pleasingly so, and consequently they stop exercising. However, they find that through neglect of diet and exercise, the tide turns, inches creep back upon their hips, and before they quite realise what is

[†]*Total Fitness*, Lawrence Moorhouse, Hart-Davies MacGibbon, 1976

happening they are back with their tight waist-bands and flabby thighs.

Weight trainers seem to be made of sterner stuff. Habits become ingrained. They are used to the idea of completing a specific programme, and of seeing progress on their record cards. And they seem less willing to lose all the gains they have made by returning to an inactive life with old habits of over-eating. Weight trainers know how to compensate for any occasional indulgence, a period of forced inactivity perhaps on holiday and with heavier meals. They are ready to cope with any surplus weight as soon as it appears on their personal records.

Do not weigh yourself more than once a fortnight and do this always at the same time, ideally shortly after rising, without your clothes and before breakfast. Body weight does fluctuate almost unaccountably so be prepared for this and don't be disappointed. You can measure yourself weekly with a tape measure but remember that changes will be gradual. The added bonus of lean muscular tissue makes you feel better. Furthermore, as most weight trainers will vouch, there comes to them all the psychological benefit that follows an energetic session with the weights. It can be as good for the mind as it is for the body; stress is replaced by serenity.

The harder muscles work, the more energy fuel they will need. At first they respond by using up their own stored supply – glycogen. During sustained physical activity, as for example in a stamina weight training circuit, the body is forced to call upon its own reserves of fat. Hormones are released to break down this adipose tissue round your hips and thighs into what is known as 'free fatty acids'. These are carried to the muscles in the blood stream and converted into energy fuel.

When you stop the rigorous exercise and have something to eat, the carbohydrates in the food are immediately used to replenish the energy stores – glycogen – in the muscles and liver. The point for slimmers to note is that if you do not eat more than you need for that replenishing process the body fat that has been used up in the exercise will not be replenished. You will have lost weight.

If you try to lose weight merely by depriving yourself of food by sticking to a very low calorie diet, then your slimming campaign could be self-defeating because your body would lose both fat and muscle. And then, because you have less muscle than before to burn up fat as energy fuel, you will need even less food to meet your body's needs. It becomes harder and harder to lose weight. So you are more likely to meet with success when you slim if you exercise and the most effective way that can be found is weight training.

CHAPTER ELEVEN Figure control – facing the facts

Women are rebelling against the conspiracy between fashion critics and designers who for so long have been dictating the shape of a woman's body. Jane Mulvagh, fashion editor of *The European* newspaper, recently fired a barrage against their power, which, she said, prevented women from buying the clothes which really suited their figures. And furthermore she declared:

> Their power does not end there. Even more pernicious is fashion's ability to distort women's bodies and alarm their sense of well-being and self-esteem. 'Curves are in!' or 'Boobs are back in Paris!' the headlines have announced over the past two years. But while a full bosom is 'in' again, what nature generally appends to such shapeliness is definitely 'out'. It has been dictated that the rest of you must remain pencil-thin. Women are bewildered – how to be large and small at the same time? Some are driven to desperate measures to keep slim.[†]

Commonsense is creeping into discussions of what really is the ideal female form. You don't need to look like a fashion model and looking fit and healthy isn't about having the perfect figure. If we give more serious thought to what is natural shapeliness in a woman's figure then we can more honestly consider what can and cannot be achieved by figure control methods.

Figure control sounds so easy when exercises are couched in fancy sales talk that trips off the tongue. We've all come across it at some time or another, those alliterative terms like the 'midriff minimiser', 'bust bracer' and 'waist whittlers'. But do they work? Can pads clamped to your problem areas really get rid of so called cellulite? And if not, can weight training do any better? These have become hotly contended issues and usually at the bottom of the hype is another product designed to separate you from your hard-earned cash. But before you pay out anything, have a look at what the medical profession has to say about the most contentious area of them all – cellulite.

[†]*The European*, Elan Supplement, 12 July 1991

What about cellulite?

The unsightly dimpled flesh gathered around the buttocks and thighs is known as cellulite. And according to recent articles in popular magazines, 80 per cent of all women 'suffer' from it. The fact that thin people have it too has led to it being considered as hormone related and that theory is backed by the plausible argument that men don't have it. Many women declare the problem gets worse just before their periods.

What, then, are those orange peel-like dimples, those stubborn areas of fat or cellulite – though this is a term never encountered a decade or so ago? Scientists say there is no such thing. Doctors have no difficulty in providing a definition: 'They are simply pockets of fat, nothing more and nothing less', is their usual answer.

Those who market sure-fire remedies for cellulite clearly have good reason to disagree; they claim that this fat is a special kind of fat – 'trapped fat', which has been established for some length of time producing 'bumpy bottoms' and 'orange-peel arms'. They say it may be caused by caffeine, by smoking, by stress, by the pill and if not that then it's probably hereditary or caused by 'hormonal disturbances'.

Dr David Fenton, a consultant dermatologist in London, argues that cellulite does not even exist:

> Cellulite is a modern term, something that's been invented by commercial companies. What I understand is that they are describing fat. What did ladies have before there was cellulite? They had fat and they still have fat. Cellulite does not really exist. The fat differs in that if you have larger stores in some areas it looks slightly different to that where you have smaller stores. If you have smaller fat deposits then you can have a smooth surface. If you have great rolls of fat not only do you have enormous layers but also you can get a slightly dimpled appearance and it can feel firmer and harder simply because you have large amounts present in the same body area.[‡]

And Dr Fenton adds that men can get 'cellulite', for instance on their backs and stomachs, if they're very overweight.

Do special diets have more effect than others on this stubborn fat? Where is the clinical evidence to support claims that a diet without tea, coffee, bread or pasta is the way to banish cellulite? Dr Martin Hughes, Lecturer in Clinical Pharmacology at Cambridge University, recently declared in the same debate on *BBC Radio Four* that he had not seen any scientifically conducted work that had shown that any one calorie-controlled diet had more effect than another. 'The question really is,' he said, 'that you must not take in more than you burn off'.

Some journalists write that cellulite comes from poisonous wastes clogging up the system. 'Pools of toxic fluid build up and become

‡*BBC Radio Four broadcast*, July 1991

trapped between the pockets', wrote Nadine Baggott in *Living Magazine*, June 1991. Dr Fenton disagrees. 'There is no medical or scientific evidence whatsoever that toxins have anything to do with it. I mean, nobody ever knows what sort of toxins these people are talking about. Fat is fat!' It's no secret what the answer to the problem is – follow a simple low calorie diet and take plenty of exercise.' There is no cream or magic potion on the market that will melt away cellulite.

Another wrongly recommended treatment is massage. Journalists write in pseudo-medical terminology about how 'a gentle but firm movement of hand over skin will aid blood delivery to the cells, oxygenating them and encouraging the lymph system to remove trapped fluid and toxic waste.' Yet at the same time others are admitting that no matter how hard you try, massage will not slim you down nor redistribute fat. You could, of course, buy a brush made from Mexican cactus fibre 'to boost your circulation to remove cellulite' the claim of manufacturers of such instruments. But before parting with your money, for these brushes are not cheap, consider the professional medical opinion that there is absolutely no scientific or medical evidence that massage will break down or remove fat cells or fat globules at all. If such procedures as body brushing or massaging, are too severe they can very easily damage the skin by excessive friction, causing bleeding, broken veins and bruising.

Weigh the scientific evidence against the myriad of marketing claims and the sensible option is clear: take effective exercise, weight training, and eat less than you burn in physical activity. That is the safe way to lose those dimples or bumps, or rolls of fat – whether you call them cellulite or not!

Now from the bottom to the top.

What can weight training do for your back and shoulders?

A dowager's hump, that flesh-covered curve at the top of the spine, is now seen more often than ever. You could just cover it up with extra clothing but happily, there is an alternative – improve it.

There are two problems to consider: Removing excess fat and the bulging dowager's hump, padding the scrawny angularities with smooth muscular curves.

Like all other problems of figure control, these must be tackled from three aspects – purposeful exercise, diet and postural correction. The dowager's hump is usually a combination of too much fat and a minor postural defect – slight kyphosis or round back. The condition of kyphosis, seen in its advanced form in elderly women, can develop very early in life – between the ages of ten and twenty. The abnormality might arise from defective vision, slight deafness, debilitating illness, overwork or bad posture. If such bad habits, started during the teenage years, are allowed to pass uncorrected, the resulting defects are more difficult to eradicate and the condition worsens.

A correct diet will soon eliminate the fat and, in the younger woman, exercise can improve the postural abnormality. But if rehabilitative therapy is delayed, bony and ligamentous changes can make the condition chronic and beyond response to exercise.

Systematic weight training exercises are a form of preventive medicine. They can rebuild muscular balance between opposing muscle groups of the upper back, chest and shoulder, and restore mobility to joints. Head carriage is automatically improved when dorsal muscles are strengthened and their habitual length shortened to normal.

For many years now Professor Arthur Watkins, Chief of Physical Medicine of Massachusetts General Hospital, and his assistant, Dr Thomas DeLorme, have been recommending the use of weight training exercises to prevent progressive kyphosis. In one of the standard works on remedial gymnastics, *Progressive Resistance Exercise* (Appleton Century Crofts, New York 1951), they write that although the degenerative condition of kyphosis 'usually causes more deformity than pain', exercises for the upper back muscles over a period of two to three months can bring about considerable improvement', which may often be maintained by teaching the patient better postural habits.

One special weight training exercise they recommend for alleviation of the condition is this: lying face downwards on a bench with the upper part of the body off the bench, a disc weight is attached to a headband round the forehead; the head and shoulders are then raised as far as possible with the chin tucked in towards the chest.

Not many gyms have such headbands but Nautilus machines such as the 4-Way Neck Exerciser provide direct or variable resistance for the trapezius muscle to work against. This muscle, often classified more as a back muscle, does in fact support the entire back of the neck. A contoured head pad on the machine keeps the head in position during the various phases of the primary movements to exercise the neck: anterior flexion, posterior extension, lateral contraction to the right and lateral contraction to the left. It is an ideal corrective exercise.

Despite the vital work the neck muscles have to do, day in, day out, they are probably the most undertrained muscles of the whole body.

Suitable exercises using free weights can be found in the dorsal exercise section of Chapter 5.

Progress towards a more balanced upper torso will depend upon the way you increase the poundage on the bar or resistance on the machine. Naturally some women will respond more quickly than others but all muscles inevitably respond beneficially to exercise. Remember, muscles make the curves and maintain graceful poise.

The relationship between your neck, head and back is the key to good poise and posture, which can make all the difference between how you look and feel. It can compensate even for a few extra pounds by presenting an impression of grace instead of heaviness.

Posture is very important; have you noticed how often, when weight training exercises are described, special attention is given to the way your back is held, and how important it is to adopt a correct position for the exercise? Partly this emphasis is for reasons of safety, but there is another reason – to make you conscious of your posture all of the time.

What is good posture?

It is difficult to describe what really constitutes good posture because the terms 'posture' and 'poise' really mean balance, and the body can be balanced in scores of different positions. You can strike a different posture for every situation; one of readiness in receiving a tennis service, a relaxed posture for sleeping, another for nursing a baby, and so on. But in order to lay down basic principles for good poise it is sometimes convenient to describe an efficient standing posture. Usually this is defined as one where an imaginary plumb line would drop centrally through the body between ears, shoulders, hips, knees and ankles.

At the same time it must be emphasised that the ideal posture is the one which provides maximum efficiency for each particular situation with minimum effort. It is one that looks right for the occasion and most women would agree that an erect, well-balanced posture gives a more elegant appearance – clothes fit better and you will feel more at ease with your body. Once you have developed good posture you will, without any apparent effort, balance gracefully all the different parts of the body one on top of the other: head and neck on the body, with a straight spine on the pelvis, and the pelvis correctly over the legs and feet.

With most young people all these parts are already perfectly poised and balanced, but gradually with the passing years we pick up bad habits that rob us of poise and consequently postural defects develop. These do not merely mar appearance but also impair performance. Think of it this way: the pelvis forms the base upon which the upper body is supported and at the same time is the power house for locomotion. Attached to it is a complex network of muscles and tendons which provide the power for walking, running, jumping, bending and turning. It is easy to see, therefore, that the pelvic musculature must be harmoniously developed and strengthened, to ensure a stable support for the body and also be a firm base from which the muscles can work as prime movers and stabilisers too.

Your upper body – a new look

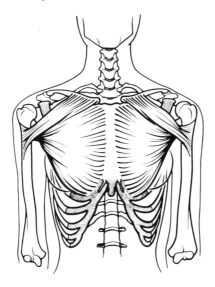

You can firm up the fan-shaped pectoral muscles which support the breasts quite easily by progressive resistance exercises. Try this test. Place your left hand over your right breast and then bring your right arm, bent at the elbow forcibly across your body, as a boxer might in punching a bag. You will feel the pectoral muscles rise up as they contract powerfully.

Weight training exercises as described in the chest section of Chapter 5 will do much to strengthen your pectoral muscles. Their fibres will become stronger and broader. New capillaries will open up to feed the muscle, the increased blood supply carries vital energy fuel and tissue building material to the working muscle. Protein from the diet is utilised for new tissue growth, and fats, also carried in the blood stream, may be deposited between the muscle fibres as well as under the skin. And so a new form begins to take shape without disturbing or irritating the delicate mammary glands.

One of the best exercises for developing the pectoral muscles is the traditional free weight bench press. Many experienced instructors stress the importance of this exercise and testify to the beneficial results. Or you could use the new Nautilus machines and especially the Decline and Incline Press. The Decline Press machine provides balanced and variable resistance as well as opportunities for independent movement of the arms. In particular it works the lower pectorals, triceps and the latissimus dorsi. Similarly the Incline Press offers variable handgrip positions and different forms of resistance to the pushing muscles of the chest and arms, which are the upper pectorals, front deltoids and triceps. With such equipment the upper and lower halves of the pectorals – which act like two separate muscles – can be given special attention.

Rehabilitation of the waistline

What polite euphemism can we use to describe that abdominal bulge – the spare tyre? Whatever its name, a protruding tummy not only looks unsightly and prevents the wearing of slim-fitting clothes, but it also has an adverse effect on general health through the displacement of the abdominal organs. These are carried in a bowl-shaped cavity. Two-thirds of the bowl is formed by pelvic bone while the front third is merely the muscular abdominal wall. If these muscles sag, the contents of the bowl slip forward and lie heavily against the weakened front wall. Their weight is partly held by the retaining tissue which attaches the viscera to the spine at the rear, but the constant drag of the fluid-filled intestines stretches the attachment until eventually the whole weight of fluids and intestines flops entirely on the inadequate muscle wall, which is far too weak to carry the extra burden. When the intestines lie in a heap, instead of snugly in their proper place, the flow of vital juices is impeded, causing digestive disorders of varying degrees. At this stage corrective treatment is urgently needed. Prevention though is far easier.

Exercises for rehabilitating the abdominal muscles

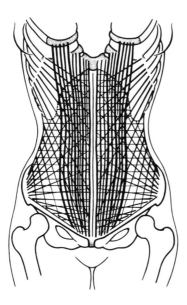

Exercise is only effective when supplemented by other measures already described – improvement of postural habits, reduction of weight by a good diet and physical activity which burns off calories. So don't expect overnight success or that being hard on yourself will speed up the process. Before you start your abdominal rehabilitation bear in mind one vital principle – **never** work abdominal muscles when they are stretched.

Do not forget that there are three main muscles to be exercised and for each there is an especially beneficial exercise. Look at the muscles shown in the diagram opposite. You should know them, for they give multi-way, elastic stretch support to your abdomen as well as providing the power to turn and twist the trunk. The most effective exercises for these muscles are the trunk curls and crunches, the trunk twisting and lowering, described in Chapter 5 and also an exercise which we have not yet discussed. It is known as the abdominal retraction or stomach lift.

Few people can manage this exercise well on the first attempt – don't give in! It is especially good for the transversalis muscle, that broad sheet shown in the diagram with horizontal lines, which has the main function of holding the abdominal contents in place. The simplest way to get the feel of this exercise is to stand slightly bent forward at the hips, place both hands on your knees, breathe out all the air in your lungs, then try to blow out more. Before you breathe again, lift your chest up still keeping your hands on your knees. Try to feel your stomach being sucked upwards inside the chest cavity. As you get more used to the feeling of achieving a hollow beneath the ribs, you will be able to do the exercise without needing to place your hands on knees or lean forward at the waist.

Finally, an essential part of the corrective weight training programme must be aimed at strengthening the dorsal muscles, which help to maintain an upright posture, and in developing the feel of a correct stance. Work at these exercises regularly and your waistline will reappear. You will look and feel much better.

CHAPTER TWELVE   The choice is yours

From the fitness boom of the 1980s there came a bewildering array of different exercise forms, backed by a barrage of scientific jargon. Not surprisingly, it was all too easy to become confused and even cynical about the various claims being made. Through it all, however, weight training emerged more popular than ever before. It really does answer positively the two most important questions for any exercise programme: first, 'Does it produce the required results?' and second, 'Can we keep it up?'

Yes! Whether weight training is done for preventive health care, getting fitter, slimmer or for improving performance in sport, the benefits are quickly and readily appreciated. All you need to do is start. Go to a gym or fitness centre. Once you start your own programme you will soon see the difference that it makes.

Understandably, when it comes to keeping fit we are inclined to ignore it, to put off for a few days, weeks, even years, the action we should take now. It is mere procrastination, foolhardy and irresponsible. But we all do it – we allow ourselves to be pushed on by the pressure of day to day events. Once you accept the fact that your fitness should be maintained, then you must pause to consider the best practical means of achieving it. Somehow you must find the time.

You have already taken the time to read this book, so why not make this part of a determined plan to do something about it. Contained within these pages is a plan suitable for you: a routine that will give you the most benefit for your efforts. You have a wide range of options to start from and you can incorporate training for whatever sport you are interested in. You are not tied to one routine; when you are ready – change it – move on. Develop! Improve! Progress!

The choice is yours. Life is not a gamble, and your well-being does not have to be left to chance. Take up the challenge. It must be met by positive action. In the final analysis you are responsible for your health, for your fitness and for making the most of it.

It is indeed, your choice!

Take up Sport

The Take up Sport series is the perfect introduction to sport, as well as explaining the basic rules each book provides hints and tips on techniques and strategy so that the newcomer can enjoy the game right from the start. Each book is written by an acknowledged expert in the sport. 210 × 100mm 48-64 pages black and white photographs and many line drawings second colour inside £2.95 Paperback

Take up Cricket	0 947655 58 1
Take up Cycle Racing	0 947655 57 3
Take up Badminton	0 947655 60 3
Take up Rugby Union	0 947655 67 0
Take up Snooker	0 947655 61 1
Take up Swimming	0 947655 70 0
Take up Soccer	0 947655 71 9
Take up Golf	0 947655 59 X
Take up Gymnastics	0 947655 62 X
Take up Sailing	0 947655 65 4
Take up Table Tennis	0 947655 66 2
Take up Tennis	0 947655 69 7
Take up Athletics	0 947655 74 3
Take up Netball	0 947655 76 X
Take up Canoeing	0 947655 83 2
Take up Judo	0 947655 77 8
Take up Squash	0 947655 72 7
Take up Rock Climbing	0 947655 84 0
Take up Basketball	0 947655 79 4
Take up Bowls	0 947655 73 5
Take up Hockey	0 947655 80 8
Take up Skiing	0 947655 68 9
Take up Weightlifting	0 947655 82 4
Take up Windsurfing	0 947655 75 1

The books can be obtained from most good booksellers or directly from

SPRINGFIELD BOOKS LTD

Norman Road, Denby Dale, Huddersfield
HD8 8TH West Yorkshire. Tel: (0484) 864955
Fax: (0484) 865443